Emma's Promise

Book 1 in the Northwoods
Adventures Series

By Amy A. Corron

PRESS

God's blessings!
Enjoy !! :)

Amy A. Corron

This book is a work of fiction. Although Atlanta, Michigan is a real place, I have taken much creative liberty with the setting for the sake of the story. All characters are figments of my imagination. Any resemblance to people living or dead is merely coincidental.

Dedicated in memory of my mother, Mary Billings, August, 1927 – June, 1997, who instilled in each one of her seven daughters a deep love and appreciation for the written word. Wish you were here to see this, Mom.

CHAPTER ONE

Emma Dawson was just unlocking the door to her "Spot of Tea" shop when she heard the distant ringing of the telephone. She fumbled with the key in the early morning darkness, finally turning the lock and hurrying inside. Flipping on the lights in the kitchen, she reached for the ancient wall phone, wondering who in the world would be calling her at 5 a.m.

"Hello?" She didn't bother with the more formal "Spot of Tea shop" greeting this early in the morning.

"Emma, dear, it's Mom." The familiar voice on the other end of the line sent a shiver of fear up Emma's slender form. "I'm sorry to call so early, but I wanted to catch you before the morning crowd hit and you got too busy."

"What is it? Is everything okay? Is Dad okay?" Emma tamped down the quick rise of panic at this unusual early morning phone call.

"Yes, yes, everything is fine here, honestly. I'm

sorry, I didn't mean to freak you out by calling so early." Emma smiled at her mother's use of the teenage term. "It's just that I knew you would be busy later and with the summer vacation season, I knew you would go to bed exhausted, so I wanted to catch you early. Actually, I'm calling to ask a favor."

"What sort of favor?" Relieved that there was no emergency to deal with, Emma began taking inventory of the muffins in the glass-fronted case by the cash register.

"Well, I got a call last night from Mabel. She and Milt are very concerned. You know, their nephew was in some sort of horrible wreck awhile back and they've given him permission to come up and stay in their cabin to recuperate."

Emma pictured the McGillis cabin. It wasn't the best place for an injured person to try and heal. The place was a total disaster! She said as much to her mother as she went into the kitchen, stretching the phone cord as far as it would go and began setting out ingredients for the morning baking.

"From what Mabel said," her mother continued, "it's not his physical injuries that are the problem anymore. I guess the accident messed up his head and he wants to come up and work on the cabin as some sort of therapy. Milt gave his blessing of course. He hasn't worked on that place in years and it's gone to wrack and ruin, I know. Anyway, what I wanted to ask is that you keep an eye on this man. Milt and Mabel think a lot of him and they are really worried. He's not going to know anyone up there and it would really put their minds at ease to know you'll be there for him. You know, be a friendly face."

"Sure, sure," Emma gave consent without a second thought. Her soft heart already ached for this stranger who obviously was suffering. "You tell Milt and Mabel that I'll stop in and welcome him to town and check in on him every once in awhile, if I get a chance. It might not be all that often though, you wouldn't believe the summer we're having up here. It's slammed with tourists already. I can't imagine what it will be like by the Fourth of July."

"That's good. It means your business is doing well." Emma was warmed by the pride in her mother's voice. "What's new in scones now?"

"Well, I'm not trying too much new there. The locals are a little wary of anything too new fangled." Emma laughed. "But the wild blueberries are in and I'm paying a couple of teenagers to pick me as many as they can. Wild Michigan blueberry muffins are a huge hit. Which reminds me, Mom, I really need to get off here and get busy." Emma looked at the clock. It was nearly five-thirty and the shop would be opening for business at seven.

"Of course sweetie, I know you have work to do. Maybe your father and I will drive up in a few weeks and I can lend you a hand."

"That would be great Mom, I would love it. You know I have plenty of room in the house, whenever you want to come up. And tell Milt and Mabel not to worry. Tell them they should come up, too. I have a cinnamon Danish that I think Milt would love. Maybe once this nephew of theirs has the cabin fixed up, they'll actually come up and use it again.

Does this guy have a name, by the way?"

"Oh yes, his name is Tyler. Tyler McGillis."

Tyler. Emma let the name sink in. It didn't sound like the name of a person with major mental problems. She shook herself. What did she think, that people with problems didn't have ordinary names like everyone else? Besides, she shouldn't be thinking that way about a person who was suffering. Emma racked her brain for several moments, trying to remember if she had ever met Milt and Mabel's nephew. She couldn't recall ever having heard of him before. Milt was in his seventies, which would make his nephew what, forty at least.

She said goodbye to her mother and hung up the phone, looking at the array of ingredients on the gleaming counters of the shop kitchen. She had baking to do, and while she set to work on the batch of lemon poppy seed muffins, she sent up a prayer for Tyler McGillis, that he would find the peace he needed in the woods of northern Michigan.

* * *

The late June sun was shining in the windshield of Tyler's black pickup truck, making him squint. He fumbled around on the seat beside him, searching for his sunglasses. He would not take his eyes off the road, even for a second. Not to change the channel on the radio, and not to look for sunglasses. His searching hand finally found the mirrored glasses and he slipped them on, just as his exit loomed ahead.

He slowed cautiously, even though traffic was

light and he had plenty of time. Ever since the accident, Tyler did everything behind the wheel of a vehicle with extreme caution, no matter how many people laid on their horns or made lewd gestures out their car windows. It had taken him two months before he could even get behind the wheel again. The task of driving 250 miles from Toledo, Ohio to Atlanta, Michigan had been almost more than he could manage. Tyler had forced himself to face the fear and walk through it. Palms sweating, he kept his eyes on the road and the speedometer steadily on 60, knowing that, just like all those sessions in physical therapy, he would come out stronger in the end.

Uncle Milt's cabin was going to be just what he needed. Tyler had never been to the place, but he had heard his aunt and uncle talk about it often enough. Their fond memories had always stirred a longing within him. Tyler could almost see the rustic log cabin, the woods, the lake.

After a month in the hospital and two more enduring grueling physical therapy, Tyler had been left at odds, rotting in his city apartment, still unable to return to work. All he had wanted was an escape. It was then he had remembered his uncle's northern hideaway and had asked if he could use the place for awhile, the whole summer most likely.

Since the wreck, Tyler had taken a leave of absence from his job. He was hoping a summer in the north woods would finally bring complete healing and he could return to the job he loved a whole man. Uncle Milt had warned him that the place needed work. It had been vacant for years and the mice and chipmunks had probably taken over. Tyler didn't mind. Hard work and solitude, that was what he wanted, what he needed. No phone, no helpful friends or family calling just to say "how you doing, buddy?"

Tyler gritted his teeth at the thought and wanted to scream. "How you doing?" How did they think he was doing? He had killed a child! Did they really think that one day they would ask him that and he would laugh and say "fine, great"? Tyler felt the haunting memories wash over him like a tidal wave, forcing him under, drowning him in a sea of regret and pain. No! He had wanted to leave the past behind in the city, not drag it along like so much unwanted baggage.

Forcing his mind to go blank, Tyler tried to concentrate on the road. Look for deer, he reminded himself. For goodness sake, don't hit any. M33 was a beautiful, winding road with roller coaster hills that passed through small towns with names like Fairview and Rose City. Under normal circumstances it would have been a pleasant, relaxing drive, but Tyler couldn't wait to get off the road. Relief flowed over him when he saw the sign for Atlanta. Not far now. And then he remembered his promise to his Aunt Mabel.

He had to stop at some shop called the Tea Pot or the Tea Spot or some such nonsense. He remembered Aunt Mabel's pleading look when he had stopped at their house last night to pick up the key to the cabin.

"Please Tyler, just stop in and check up on the girl. Her name is Emma and her parents are our dearest friends. We've all been a little worried about her, living alone in the north woods like she does. And running that shop all by herself. Well, anything could happen. We pray for her every day, but it would really set our minds to rest if you would just peek in at her. Just stop in and say hello from Milt and Mabel. You will do that for us, won't you?" Aunt Mabel had put a frail, liver spotted hand to her heart and gazed at Tyler with such an imploring look, that of course he had agreed to stop in and say hello on his way to the cabin.

A grimace twisted Tyler's handsome features, pulling the scar on his cheek tight. The last thing on earth he wanted to do was stop in at some stuffy tea shop and make small talk with a stranger. Worse, a woman! Since getting out of the hospital, Tyler had avoided as much human contact as possible, even with his own family. He saw the way people looked at him. His family, with pity. But the general public, their looks seemed to scream "Freak!" It would take as much courage for Tyler to introduce himself to a stranger as it had for him to drive the last 250 miles.

Tyler let out a long sigh. Oh well, he had promised to stop in and say hello. It was the least he could do for his aunt and uncle, for the use of their cabin for the summer. And wasn't that what this trip was all about, healing and facing his fears? Aunt Mabel's concern for this Emma was genuine, so what was five minutes of his time? Once he did his duty, he was off the hook. He could let Aunt Mabel know that their friend's daughter was fine and he could go about his business at the cabin, which was no business at all.

Just what he needed for the summer.

The road sign said he was entering the Atlanta Corporate limits, "Elk Capital of Michigan." Tyler eased off the gas, slowing to a snail's pace as he looked for the tea shop. East side of town, Uncle Milt had said, before you hit the turn to the cabin. Tyler spotted it. "Spot of Tea Shop" was elegantly painted in calligraphy on a sign in front of a low building painted light lavender with white gingerbread trim.

He signaled a left-hand turn and pulled into the parking lot that was nearly full of vehicles. Several moments passed as Tyler stared at the building, fighting the familiar anxiety. Sheer force of will made him swipe his sweating palms across jean clad thighs, take a deep breath and open the door.

Emma rang up Kelly Clark's order of two dozen muffins. It was a familiar routine since Kelly stopped in every day for the same order, which she offered to her customers at Kelly's Kut and Kurl while they were getting their permanents or color highlights.

"Really, Em, I wish you would make an appointment and let me do something with your hair," Kelly said as the tiny bell over the door gave a warning tinkle. Emma looked up to see a tall, blond stranger enter the Spot of Tea.

It wasn't unusual to have a stranger walk into the shop. A good portion of Emma's business came from tourists stopping in during their vacations. But something about this man made Emma pause and look him over more carefully, from the top of his dark blond hair, to the vivid scar that ran across his forehead and down his cheek. There were deep lines etched around his moss green eyes. Those eyes. What was it about those eyes? Emma wondered, not hearing Kelly as she prattled on about the latest hairstyles and colors. Haunted. That was it. Those green eyes that looked around her shop were haunted.

"So, do you want me to set you up an appointment, Em?" Kelly asked, bringing Emma's mind back to her customer with a yank. "I think a little highlights would do wonders for you."

"Not right now, Kelly. I just don't have time for fooling with my hair during summer season." Emma ran a hand over her dark hair in its French braid. A few strands had come loose and she self-consciously tucked them up. "I appreciate the offer and I promise I'll come in for a trim soon. Maybe next week. I have to think about color though. Maybe I could do that in the fall, when things slow down."

"But Emma, fall isn't the time for highlights! Summer is when you want to put those golden glints in your hair. Then it looks natural, like bleaching from the sun."

Emma watched the scarred stranger move forward among the antique tables and chairs, crowded with customers. Her waitress, Rhonda, rushed between the kitchen and the dinning room, filling orders. Emma really had no more time to talk about her hair!

"I'll think about it Kelly and give you a call, I promise," Emma tried to politely dismiss one of her best customers as the man with the tormented gaze stepped forward. Kelly's attention was momentarily diverted by the blond giant standing next to her. She stopped talking about Emma's hair and gave the newcomer one of her best homecoming queen smiles. His eyes though were riveted on Emma, so Kelly grabbed her bag of muffins, leaving the shop in a huff.

"Can I help you?" Emma had to look up, up, to meet his eyes. A hand came up and brushed his dark gold hair back off his forehead, leaving the pinkish white scar more visible. Then, as if suddenly aware of what he had done, he brushed it back forward, partially covering the marred skin.

"Are you Emma?" he asked abruptly.

"Yes," Emma answered slowly. What on earth had she done now? Her mind quickly scanned back. Had she paid her taxes? Were all her utilities paid up? Was she due for an inspection? "Is there something I can do for you?"

"Actually, I'm Tyler McGillis. My Aunt Mabel asked me to stop in and say hello from her and Uncle Milt. I'm staying at their cabin for the summer."

"Oh, yes!"

Emma's mind spun with surprise. This was the nephew! The troubled man who needed to heal. No wonder his eyes had that haunted look about them. And the scar on his face, evidence of the accident her mother had spoken of. But the mental picture she had drawn had not been at all accurate! Emma's whole being quivered with awareness of the man in front of her cash register.

"But you're so young!" she blurted without

thinking. Embarrassment immediately warmed her cheeks.

A small smile nearly turned up a corner of Tyler's mouth and the pain seemed to recede somewhat from his gaze as he watched Emma try to regain her composure.

"My father is the youngest in their family, Uncle Milt is the oldest. Since there were ten kids, there was quite an age difference."

"Oh, oh, I see." Flustered, Emma tried to regain her dignity. "It's nice to meet you. How are Milt and Mabel?"

"They're fine. I just told them I would stop in and say hello from them." His eyes scanned the crowded shop and his unease returned. "I can see you're really busy, and that's all I was supposed to do anyway." He looked ready to bolt out the door.

"Wait! Here, take these with you." Shaking off the embarrassment, and the befuddled feelings Tyler's presence was causing, Emma began filling a white sack with muffins and scones from the glass fronted case. "You're going to need all the sustenance you can get, working on that cabin."

Tyler reached for his wallet as she held the full sack out to him. Emma shook her dark head. "No, on the house. Consider it a welcome to town present. And insurance for future business." She smiled, wishing she could wipe away the pain that was so deeply etched on his face. Their hands brushed as Tyler took the bag from her, sending an electric current through her fingertips.

"Thanks, well, it was nice meeting you." Tyler

backed toward the door, nearly toppling an elderly lady in his haste. "Sorry ma'am." Tyler reached to steady the woman then nodded toward Emma once more before bolting out the door, setting the silver bell to tinkling with a vengeance.

Emma stood motionless, watching a black pickup truck pull out of the parking lot and head toward town. She caught a glimpse of blond hair and mirrored sunglasses as the truck drove down the street. What was Tyler trying to get away from so quickly? Emma wondered. Was it her or was something more sinister chasing him?

"Emma!" Rhonda's frantic voice called from the kitchen, shaking her out of her reverie. Customers were waiting. Thoughts of Tyler McGillis were going to have to wait until later.

CHAPTER TWO

Tyler drove slowly through town, trying to shake the picture of Emma from his mind. The petite brunette was seared into his brain after only brief moments with her. Those knowing hazel eyes had seemed to look straight into his soul, and when their hands had brushed, Tyler had felt something spring to life inside him. She had not cringed in revulsion at the sight of his disfigured face. She had smiled with a warmth that wrapped around him. Tyler couldn't fathom why his aunt was so concerned. Emma Dawson appeared to be perfectly fine. A little too perfect, maybe.

He smiled at the thought of her blurted comment about his age. Obviously she had been warned he was coming and wasn't what she had expected. He had to admit, she wasn't quite what he had imagined, either.

Not liking the road his thoughts were traveling down, Tyler turned his mind instead to the town he was driving through. There were the normal small town shops, real estate offices, a hardware store and gas station. All on Main Street with one blinking light in the center of town. A far cry from the crowded city he had left just this morning.

Turning at the blinker, Tyler headed the truck south on the county road that led to his uncle's cabin. The pavement soon turned to dirt and in less than a mile Tyler saw the sign for Ryan Road. He made a left hand turn, driving slowly over the rough sand and rock. Around a curve and there was the overgrown drive to his uncle's place on the right. It was nothing more than an overgrown two track with knee high weeds down the middle. Going at a turtle's pace, Tyler crept the truck up the lane and stopped in front of the derelict cabin.

His eyes widened at the sight. The screened in porch that went across the front of the cabin was in tatters. The door hung at an odd angle. Mice and chipmunks, huh? It looked as if more than small rodents had inhabited the place over the past several years. He cringed at the thought of what he would find inside.

The screen door squeaked in loud protest as Tyler opened it and walked across the wooden porch floor strewn with leaves and other debris. The lock in the heavy wood door into the cabin took muscle to turn, and for a brief moment Tyler thought it wasn't going to budge. Finally the knob turned in his hand and the door swung inward, revealing more of the same that was on the porch.

The large, rectangular room was a mess. Animal droppings were everywhere, the air musty from going too long without any circulation. Something scurried in a dark corner of the loft above. Tyler looked up then back down at the floor. A rotted out spot in the wooden planks attested to the leak he could clearly see when he looked up at the steeply pitched roof. He walked over to the stone fireplace. Rodents were nesting in the iron cavity, meaning the chimney was probably clogged. His uncle had certainly underestimated the amount of "fixing up" the place needed! Well, he had come here to get away from it all, to clear his mind of nightmarish thoughts and put his body to physical labor. No doubt he was getting just that!

There was little furniture in the cabin, and what had been left had become food for wood chewing rodents or nests for other small creatures. A wooden table and chairs still stood in the corner that passed for a kitchen. Tyler hated to think what was nesting in the bowels of the old refrigerator and stove. A hand pump over the sink reminded him that he was roughing it.

A short hallway led to a bedroom at the back of the cabin, in no better shape than the rest of the place. A second door opened into a room that obviously was going to be a bath, had Uncle Milt ever gotten around to finishing it. A commode and sink lay on the floor where they had been left, uninstalled, for more years than Tyler wanted to think about.

He ran his hands through his hair and over his face, momentarily closing his eyes to the disaster around him. Maybe it was all a mirage, he thought, a trick of his tired mind. It wasn't really that bad. Tyler opened his eyes and looked around once more. Yes, it really was that bad. With a heavy sigh, he headed out to his truck to unload his supplies and start on the daunting task of making his uncle's cabin habitable for more than just woodland creatures.

The Spot of Tea closed at four o'clock. It was then, after the doors were closed, that Emma counted the day's receipts, took inventory of supplies and baked goods, decided on new recipes to try, and cleaned up from the day's business. Rhonda stayed and helped clean the tables and wash the antique dishes that were used to serve the eat-in customers. All part of the quaint, Victorian ambience Emma had created in her little shop.

Today was no different. Rhonda was in the back carefully washing the mismatched plates, cups and saucers as Emma sat at one of the antique tables out front, tallying the cash register receipts. She looked up in surprise when Rhonda plopped down in the chair across from her.

"So, are you going to tell me who that man was?" Rhonda's blue eyes shone with curiosity.

"What man? We must have had at least fifty men in here today. Which one are you talking about?" Emma purposely looked back down at the calculator in front of her.

"Come on Em, the tall guy with the blond hair and the scar. The one you stood staring after for a good five minutes after he drove away, leaving me to wait on everyone by myself. I'm sure you remember. We may have had fifty men in here today, but that guy left the biggest impression! And I don't recall you staring all doe eyed after any of the others." Rhonda sat back in the fragile chair and tucked a few strands of her wayward red hair back into its ponytail.

"I did not stare doe eyed after anyone, Rhonda Weaver. And if you must know, the man you are talking about is Milt and Mabel's nephew, Tyler. He's staying out at the McGillis place for the summer." Emma tried to concentrate on the figures in front of her. "He just stopped in to say hello from Milt and Mabel."

"He's staying out at that decrepit cabin?" Rhonda asked, repressing a shiver. "Does he have any idea what he's getting into or is he some sort of roughing it wilderness freak? That place will probably fall down around his ears if a storm blows in."

Emma shrugged a slim shoulder, unwilling to divulge too much personal information about Tyler. Atlanta was a small town. It wouldn't be long before everyone knew Tyler was staying at the McGillis cabin. But his reasons for being there were his own and not fodder for the town gossip mill.

"I think he plans to work on fixing the place up," was all Emma would say. "Are the dishes done in the back? If they are, you can go home." She didn't look up at Rhonda again. She didn't want her good friend to see the gamut of emotions that were running through her at the thought of Tyler. She couldn't grasp the depth of his suffering, but the demons in his soul must be great if he had to escape to that run down cabin trying to get away from them.

It was well after six when Emma locked up the shop and walked the short distance to the bank on the corner to make her deposit in the night drop box. She drank deeply of the northern Michigan air with its distinctive "up north" scent. How she wished she could bottle up that smell and sell it to the tourists! Nothing else on earth smelled like up north.

The town was still bustling with traffic heading out of town toward the many lakes and campgrounds that were spread over the area. Most of the shops on Main Street were closed, but the gas station on the corner was still doing brisk business, and the restaurants were full with the dinner crowd. Emma looked both ways before dashing across the busy thoroughfare towards her house.

She had purchased the old Victorian home the same year she opened The Spot of Tea Shop. It was a mere block off the main road but seemed more remote. It was set back on its large lot and surrounded by huge, old trees that shaded the wrap around porch. Vacant for several years before Emma purchased it, the house had taken many hours of back breaking labor to restore it to its former glory. Three years ago the yard had been a mass of overgrown weeds. Now brightly colored flowerbeds edged the deep green carpet of lush grass and graced the walkway that led from the sidewalk up to the front door.

Emma stopped a moment to admire the house. She sent up a quick prayer of thanks for her home. It really was a dream come true. God was so good, Emma thought, as she unlocked the gleaming black front door and headed into the cool interior of the house toward the kitchen.

As Emma poured herself a tall glass of lemonade, her eyes fell on the wall phone. Should she call her mother and tell her that she had met Milt and Mabel's nephew? But what would she say? "I met Tyler McGillis?" There wasn't much more to it than that. Well, she could say, "I met Tyler McGillis and he made my heart pound like I had just run the fifty yard dash."

Emma nearly giggled at the thought, then remembered her embarrassing outburst. The man probably thought her a complete ninny.

Toeing out of her white sneakers and peeling off her white anklets, Emma picked up her lemonade and padded barefoot back out to the front porch, plopping down on the green wicker settee in the shade. The color of the patio furniture immediately reminded Emma of Tyler's eyes. So green, so haunted.

Her mood turned serious. What was he doing now? she wondered, out there in that cabin that didn't even have running water? Emma couldn't even imagine the shape the place was in. Milt and Mabel had kept it up for years but had stopped coming up when Milt suffered his first heart attack five years ago. Emma drove back to the cabin from time to time, to keep an eye on things and make sure no vagrants decided to take up residence, and it seemed to fall further into disrepair with each visit.

What should she do? Emma wondered. What was her purpose concerning Tyler McGillis? And why couldn't she get his eyes out of her mind? The deep sadness she had seen in them had struck a chord in Emma's tender heart. What could she do to help him?

Help him. The thought shot into her mind. Yes, Tyler was going to need help if he was to get that cabin in any kind of shape to live in this summer. Would he even be able to clean it up enough to sleep there tonight?

Is that what I should do Lord? Emma prayed. *Should I go out and help Tyler clean up that cabin? But what if he doesn't want my help?*

What had her mother said? That Tyler's head was messed up and he wanted to fix the cabin up as some sort of therapy. Maybe he wouldn't appreciate her offer.

Emma remembered what Jesus had said in the book of Matthew. "Inasmuch as you did it to one of the least of these My brethren, you did it to Me." Her mind was made up. She would offer her assistance. If he sent her away, at least she had tried. With determination, Emma went back into the house and changed into cut off jean shorts and an old T-shirt before gathering an armload of cleaning supplies.

Hard work to tire the body and numb the mind. If that was what Tyler had been looking for, then he had found it at his uncle's cabin. In the hours since arriving, he had drug all the furniture out to the front lawn with its overgrown weeds. Thankfully, Aunt Mabel had armed him with a good broom, bucket, mop, rags and enough cleaning fluids to peel the paint off his truck. He had put them all to good use.

After dragging everything outside, he had swept

and mopped and emptied all the cupboards. Unfortunately all the linens and towels that had been left in the cabin were useless, eaten full of holes by moths and other critters. There wasn't much left that was useable and Tyler was glad he had brought a sleeping bag and a few other necessities. Tomorrow he would definitely be taking a trip to town for more supplies.

He stood in the yard in the fading June sun, surveying what was left of the furniture. He had peeled off his T-shirt long ago, and now stood bare chested, covered with sweat and grime. He no longer looked at the roadmap of scars that criss crossed his chest and ran down his left arm. Just as when he looked in the mirror he avoided looking at the scar on his face. Constant reminders of a past he wanted to forget, but which he would carry with him for the rest of his life. Just punishment, he figured, for what he had done.

Shaking his head to clear it of unwanted memories, Tyler walked toward his truck and the cooler in the back. He needed a cold drink and a few minutes of sitting in the shade. As he passed the driver's side door he glanced in the window and saw the white sack filled with muffins still sitting on the seat. What had Emma said? That he would need all the sustenance he could get working on this place? That was an understatement! Tyler nabbed an ice cold can of pop from the cooler in the back of his truck then opened the door far enough to grab the sack off the front seat. Carrying both, he headed down the overgrown trail that led to the lake.

As he emerged from the trees, his breath was cut

off sharply by the sight that met his eyes. The surface of the lake was smooth as glass, reflecting the clear blue sky and surrounding trees like a mirror. As Tyler stopped, he saw a fish jump out of the water a short distance from shore.

Peace. Quiet. It stole over him, soothing like balm on a ragged wound. He walked the last few steps to the water's edge and plopped down on the grassy shore. He popped the can's tab and took a long, refreshing drink as his eyes scanned around the lake. He drank in the serenity as he had the soft drink. It quenched a different type of thirst inside him.

Far across the lake a few cabins were visible, but no people were about. If there were fishermen out on the lake, he couldn't see them from this secluded spot of shore. From here it was as if he were the only person on earth. For the first time in three months, Tyler began to relax. He felt a good kind of tired. Maybe tonight he would sleep without nightmares.

He reached for the white sack and opened it, looking inside at the different sweets Emma had given him. He chose a huge muffin and looked at the little white sticker before unwrapping it. Chocolate chip. He hadn't known there was any such thing as chocolate chip muffins. Tyler took a large bite, surprised at the taste, which sent his mouth watering. He chewed slowly, enjoying the confection and the peaceful surroundings. After finishing the first muffin, he reached in the bag for another, this one labeled wild Michigan blueberry. One bite told him one thing about Emma Dawson, she sure could bake.

CHAPTER THREE

The sun set slowly, sending out shafts of pink and orange light which were reflected on the glassy surface of the lake. Tyler knew he had sat for far too long. There was much more work to be done before dark fell completely but he was loath to disturb the tranquility of this moment. As he rose to his feet he heard the low rumble of a car engine which seemed to stop up by the cabin. A door slammed.

Tyler automatically tensed. Uncle Milt had told him the townspeople were mostly friendly but Tyler didn't relish having to introduce himself to some nosey neighbor, explain what he was doing here. Silently he made his way back up the path. A slim form in cut off jeans was standing in the yard examining the run down cabin, shading her eyes with one hand. Emma Dawson. Tyler sucked in a sharp breath, feeling like someone had kicked him in the gut. She caught sight of him emerging from the path and moved his way.

"Hi Tyler."

As she approached, Emma's gaze fell to his bare chest and its criss cross of pink and white scars. She quickly looked away from his mutilated body and met his hard stare.

"I'm sorry to show up uninvited." Emma clasped her hands in front of her. "I thought maybe you could use some help. I haven't been out here in awhile, but last time I was, it wasn't a pretty sight. Looks like it was worse than I imagined, huh?" She motioned toward the refuse in the clearing in front of the cabin.

"Thanks, but I'm fine." Tyler shoved past her and walked quickly to the bed of his pickup where he retrieved his T-shirt, pulling it on over his head to cover his scars.

Tyler refused to look her in the eye. It was embarrassing, having a virtual stranger see the lasting evidence of his nightmarish past. You would think he would have gotten used to it by now, considering all the doctors, nurses and therapist who had seen his disfigured body in the past three months. But having Emma see it, for some reason that was different, hurt just a little more. At one time Tyler had been pretty proud of his physique, had even posed for the fireman's calendar last year. Now he just wanted to hide himself from the world's prying eyes.

Avoiding Emma's gaze, Tyler instead looked down at her feet in their hiking boots. As if with a will of their own, his eyes traveled up her shapely bare legs in their cut off jeans with the ragged threads hanging down her thighs. Catching himself, he forced himself to meet her eyes, ready to see the revulsion there.

Something clutched his chest tight and squeezed. The hazel eyes that looked up into his were steady, showing no pity or disgust. Instead Tyler saw gentle understanding, and something just a bit more that he couldn't quite name. She smiled and his heart leapt. Alarm bells, sounding much like the fire alarm at his old station house, rang in his head.

No good, his conscience warned him. Back off! Don't get too close to this one. You're only here for the summer, remember, to get well so you can return to work. Unconsciously he backed a step away from her.

"Like I said, I'm fine," Tyler's voice was hard as he steeled himself against this unexpected and unwanted reaction to her. "I've, um, made a lot of progress already. But thanks for the offer though." He turned his back on her and walked toward the cabin, but could tell she was following a few steps behind.

"You're sure I can't help?" Emma's voice held a note of disappointment. "Have you eaten anything? I brought some sandwiches. I didn't know what you would have with you. I can't have Milt and Mabel thinking I let you starve out here."

Tyler stopped amid the discarded furniture and debris in the yard and began sorting through the trash.

"No, thanks. I, um, actually, I just ate some of those muffins you gave me. They, um, they were good." He continued to avoid looking at her, hating himself and the way he tripped over his words. Why didn't she just get in her little blue sedan and drive away?

"I'm glad you liked them." Emma smiled and headed toward her car.

For a brief moment Tyler thought she was leaving. His heart sank when she merely opened the back door of her car and pulled out a large bucket filled with supplies. She left the bucket on the ground and took from it a box of lawn and garden bags. Opening the box, she pulled out a huge black bag as she walked back to the pile at Tyler's feet. Without a word she began shoving refuse in the bag. Seconds passed as Tyler watched her in disbelief. Then, he too took a bag from the box and wordlessly began to clean up the mess he had left in the yard.

They worked side by side for several minutes, Tyler trying to figure what to do about the woman who was disrupting his heartbeat. She had obviously recovered from her slip of the tongue this morning. Now it was his turn to get a grip on himself!

When most of the small items had been shoved into garbage bags and deposited in the back of Tyler's truck to be taken to the dump, Emma began sorting through the odds and ends of furniture.

"It doesn't look like there's much here you can salvage." Emma tossed a tattered cushion from the couch onto the pile of garbage in the truck bed and went back to examining the other furniture.

The bed set was a complete loss. He would be better off, for the time being, to sleep on the hard floor than on that ratty and sagging mattress and box springs. The only thing not totally destroyed was the small table and chairs, and a dresser from the bedroom that was still useable, though it could use a good coat of paint.

Emma picked up the two chairs and headed inside with them, leaving Tyler no choice but to follow her with the table. The smell of pine scented cleanser hung heavy in the air. Tyler set the table down in the kitchen area. Emma slid a chair on either side then looked around the cabin. It was dark with only the door letting in light. Plywood still covered the windows.

"I haven't been in here in years," Emma's voice was wistful and echoed slightly as she moved around the empty room. "This brings back a lot of memories."

She spoke with the same fondness that his Uncle Milt and Aunt Mabel had, obviously remembering good times shared. Tyler felt a quick stab of pain and jealousy. Where were his good memories? he wondered. It was as if his entire life had been com-pacted into a single moment in time and all he could recall was his life shattering, like splintering glass.

Emma looked across the room at him, her smile slowly fading. Giving a small shrug, she quietly left the cabin, returning moments later with an armload of clean towels and a small soft-sided cooler, which she deposited, on the table.

"I brought you some towels and stuff. I wasn't sure what you would bring and now I'm glad I thought of it, since all the ones left here were use-less. Don't worry about returning any of this, it's all extras I had around the house." Tyler's continued silence finally unnerved her enough to tie up her tongue. She looked at him, bewildered. "I brought some pots and pans, too. Do you need them?"

Tyler shook his blond head and finally spoke. "No, I think I'm set." His deep voice still held an edge of gruffness. "Aunt Mabel sent a lot of stuff up, and I brought a few things. If I need anything else, I can go buy it."

"There will be a lot of garage sales going on this time of year, you can probably pick up a few furnishings pretty cheap. And there's always the Trader, it's a free paper you can get anywhere in town, full of ads of things for sale." Tyler just nodded again, not encouraging conversation. "Are you hungry now? I've got those sandwiches in this cooler."

Her delicate, china doll looks masked the tenacity of a bulldog. Tyler finally gave a small shadow of a smile. Silence and rude behavior weren't going to dissuade her. Prickly porcupine quills were not going to hold her at bay. All the tricks he had used for the past few months to keep nurses and therapists and even his family at arms length weren't working. He didn't know if he was just tired of fighting, or maybe just ready for a new start, but somehow Emma Dawson was waltzing right through all his defenses.

As if a blindfold had been removed from his eyes, Tyler saw clearly the person he had become. Since the accident all his energy had gone toward protecting himself. He had numbed himself to all feeling and justified his obnoxious behavior as self-preservation. Now here he was, doing the same thing to Emma, when all she had done was reach out to him in kindness. His mother had raised him better, and Aunt Mabel would be appalled if she knew how he was treating the daughter of her best friend.

The scars on his body ran deep. Had they totally cut off his ability to treat people civilly? For the first time, Tyler admitted to himself that he was lonely. Holding people at bay took strength that he didn't have anymore. And he wasn't sure he wanted to. He had come here for a fresh start. Emma was offering friendship. That seemed like as good a start as any.

"Sure, that sounds good." Tyler finally accepted. "I've got some pop out in the cooler. Wait here while I go bring it in." He moved past her and out the door. Emma held open the screen as he carried the large red cooler inside.

"I hope to have the electricity on by tomorrow, but I don't know what kind of shape the refrigerator will be in," Tyler said as he placed the cooler on the floor of the kitchen, his newfound insight loosening his tongue. Looking around the room, he saw how dark it had become inside, with the windows boarded up. "I'll need to get the plywood off those windows tomorrow, too. Would you like to go outside and eat? We could head down to the lake."

"That sounds nice." Emma blessed him with one of her dazzling smiles.

She picked up her soft-sided cooler, going out in front of him and heading down the path to the lake with easy familiarity. Tyler followed behind, trying not to notice the sway of her slim hips or the curly wisps of dark hair that had escaped her long braid. At the end of the trail Emma stopped abruptly. Tyler bumped her from behind. Awareness sizzled in the cool evening air. At her quick intake of breath, he reached for her, worried, but at her sigh of pleasure he withdrew his hand and backed a step away.

"I forgot how beautiful this spot is." She smiled at him over her shoulder, seemingly unaware of the affect she was having on his insides.

She proceeded to the lake's shore and easily dropped down to the grass. As Tyler sat down a short distance from her, Emma handed him a thick sandwich swathed in plastic. Before he could begin unwrapping it, she bowed her head and said a simple prayer out loud.

"Lord, I thank you for this food. I ask your blessing upon it and upon those of us who eat it. I ask, Father, that you bless Tyler and his time here. Amen."

Tyler sat frozen during the brief prayer, not even thinking to close his eyes. When was the last time he had said a prayer over a meal? Christmas dinner with his family, probably. Along with everything else that had gone dead inside him, Tyler's faith had shriveled up and died in the accident, too. He no longer believed in prayer, but here was Emma, talking to God like she was talking to an old friend.

Unaware of his thoughts, Emma smiled and began unwrapping her sandwich. Tyler shook himself and did the same. He bit into the homemade bread and was surprised to find this was no plain and ordinary sandwich, but one stuffed to overflowing with ham, roast beef, cheeses, lettuce and tomato and tangy dressing. He couldn't stop a grunt of appreciation as he chewed and was rewarded with another of Emma Dawson's heart stopping smiles.

It was nearly dark when Emma drove out of the overgrown two track and out onto the road that led back to town. The dashboard clock read 9:30 and she realized that she still had to shower. Five a.m. comes awfully early. But she was glad she had followed the Lord's leading. She had done the right thing, reaching out a hand to Tyler McGillis, whether he had wanted it or not, which he obviously did not!

Emma thought about the scars that ran across his chest and face, and wondered how he had gotten them. What had happened in that accident? She had been sorry when he donned his T-shirt, covering up that muscular expanse of bare flesh. The brief glimpse of his chest had set her heart tripping over itself again and she had berated herself for her reaction.

Doe eyes. Rhonda's words came back to haunt her. Is that how she had looked at Tyler's chest? His discomfort had been palatable and she understood his need to hide his injuries. She remembered his hard green eyes and how they had bored into hers when she looked up from his chest. What had he been thinking right then? What kind of pain did his anger mask?

The town of Atlanta was dark and quiet as Emma drove through, only the streetlights illuminating the night and casting shadows into corners. She passed the township park and the deer pole where every fall hunters displayed their trophy bucks, and then she was through the stoplight and pulling into her narrow drive.

The headlights cut an arc through the darkness as she pulled the car into her driveway. The delicate hairs on the back of Emma's neck stood on end and a shiver ran up her spine as a shadowy form seemed to drift around the corner of her house. Emma's heart was suspended in her throat until the moon came out from behind a cloud and she laughed at herself.

Jumping at shadows passing over the moon. Really! She had lived alone here in town three years now and had never had one reason to worry about her safety. *Fear not, for I am with you*, whispered on the breeze as Emma got out of the car and went into her dark house.

After showering, Emma sat crossed legged on the bed in her upstairs bedroom in an over large T-shirt, slowly brushing out her wet hair. She looked to the telephone on the bedside table, and without a second thought picked up the receiver and dialed her parent's number. Her mother answered on the third ring.

"Hi mom, it's me," Emma said.

"Oh, Emma dear, I didn't expect to hear from you so late. Is something wrong?" Emma's mother sounded much like Emma herself had early that morning.

"No, I just wanted to let you know I met the nephew today."

"Ooh," her mother drew out the word. "And how was he?" Carolynn couldn't mask her curiosity.

"He's, well…" Emma hesitated, trying to find the right words to describe Tyler McGillis. Incredibly handsome, virile, aloof, any of them would fit. "He's distant," she finally said. "He came into the shop on his way to the cabin, to say hello from Milt and Mabel." Emma giggled, remembering her faux pas. "I totally embarrassed myself because I was expecting, you know, someone *older*, but he's not. He's maybe thirty at the most, and when he introduced himself as Milt's nephew I told him he couldn't be because he's too young! Later, after I closed up, I drove out there to see if he needed any help."

"And did he?" Carolynn sounded intrigued.

"Well, he did, but it was obvious he didn't want any. That place really is a mess, Mom. I don't think Milt realized the full extent of it. I pitched in and helped him clean up a little, even though I could tell he would rather I was a million miles away from him. He's…" Emma hesitated again, picturing the scars that covered Tyler's body. For some reason she didn't want her mother to know about that. It seemed too private and personal.

"He's what?" her mother coaxed.

"Oh, I don't know. One minute he's all stickers and burrs, the next he lets his guard down and you get a glimpse of a really nice guy. Whatever happened in that accident, he's in a lot of pain from it. Not physically, but it's there, in his eyes. I don't think he knows the Lord. I took some sandwiches out there and when I said a blessing before we ate, you should have seen the look on his face. I feel he really needs our prayers, Mom. Will you be praying for him, too?"

"Of course I will. But honey, be careful. I know he's Milt and Mabel's blood kin, but even they've been worried about him since that accident. Mabel says he just isn't himself anymore. You can't be sure what state of mind he's in."

"Mother! Aren't you the one who called me this morning and asked me to befriend him? Now you're sounding like he's some sort of mental case!"

"No, no, I don't mean it that way," Carolynn softened her tone. "I do want you to be a friendly face for him, help him out if he needs it, and wants it. But if he wants to be left alone, then maybe you should just leave it at that. You're too tender hearted for your own good."

Her mother's words from earlier that morning danced across Emma's mind. She had said that Tyler was messed up in the head. Could she be right? He had seemed like a man in pain, angry, but dangerous? Emma honestly didn't think so.

For a moment Emma wished she had never picked up the phone to call her mother. She felt disloyal discussing Tyler behind his back. Yes, he had been standoffish, even rude, but Emma had glimpsed a crack in his defensiveness and behind that wall stood a man she somehow knew was good and trustworthy. A man seeking peace. She wouldn't allow her mother's doubts to plant seeds in her mind.

"Mom, I think you've got it all wrong, but I'm too tired to argue with you," Emma's voice held an edge of stubbornness that her parents were all too familiar with. "All I'm asking is that you be praying for him, okay. Whatever happened in that accident, whatever memories are haunting him, he's going to need the Lord to get past it."

Emma heard Carolynn's contrite sigh come over the phone wire.

"Yes honey, of course your father and I will be praying for him. Now it's late and you have to get up early in the morning, so we had better say good bye for now."

"Okay Mom, thanks. Give my love to Dad and I'll call again soon."

When their good-byes were said, Emma slowly hung up the phone and plopped back against the pillows. Immediately her mind was filled with a picture of Tyler and the scars that covered his body. But what scars lay hidden deep behind those cold, hard eyes? she wondered. She pictured him in that dark cabin in the woods filled with mice and spiders and not even a mattress to sleep on.

Be with him Lord, give him rest, she prayed. "He leads me beside the still waters. He restores my soul." The words of the twenty-third Psalm brought instant comfort. *Yes Lord, that's what Tyler needs. There beside the quiet lake, restore his soul.*

Emma put down her hairbrush and switched off the lamp by her bed. Within moments she had drifted into a peaceful sleep filled with dreams of a green eyed stranger.

CHAPTER FOUR

The rising sun was just beginning to tint the eastern sky with shades of pink as Emma bustled about the tea shop's kitchen. This was her favorite time of day, when she had the shop all to herself. She loved the fragrant smells coming from the wall oven. It was like her own little cocoon, snug and warm, safe and secure. Insistent knocking on the glass of the kitchen door interrupted her solitude.

Through the glass she could make out the form of Nate Sweeney, Montmorency County Sheriff's Deputy. She hurried forward to unlock the door and let him in.

"Hey Nate, you're by early. Want a cup of coffee to keep you awake for the rest of your shift?" Emma immediately turned to the large coffee maker that was adding its own aroma to the air.

"No, actually Emma, I'm not here for coffee." The seriousness in his tone had Emma spinning back to face him, her heart thudding with dread.

"What's happened?" she asked.

"Well, I hate having to be the one to tell you this…" he hesitated, not meeting Emma's gaze.

"Just spit it out, Nate!"

"Okay." Nate nodded and took a deep breath before rushing on. "There was some vandalism last night, right outside your house. Someone spray painted your fence, and the sidewalk and the stop sign."

"Oh, that's all?" Emma dropped the hand from over her heart, relieved. "You about gave me a heart attack over some spray paint? If it's just my fence that will be easy enough to fix. It was probably some kid doing it on a dare."

"Maybe, but Emma, you need to know. The graffiti had a message, and it was addressed to you."

Gray light filtered through the chinks in the cabin and the hole in the roof, and through the grimy windows of the front door, bringing Tyler slowly awake. He rolled over in his sleeping bag on the hard wooden floor and immediately spied a chipmunk sitting up on the hearth of the fireplace, looking him over. Tyler couldn't help but smile.

"Good morning, little fella. Where's the rest of the gang?" Tyler knew there were plenty more about. He had heard the scurrying of little feet during the night. Obviously it was going to take more than sweeping to convince the small animals that this was no longer the chipmunk motel. At the sound of a voice, the chipmunk darted into the fireplace grate.

Crossing his hands beneath his head, Tyler

looked up at the patch of sky visible through the hole in the roof and sighed. Then it hit him. For the first time since the accident, he had slept without nightmares. No dreams at all that he could remember, except for a vague recollection of a dark haired vision with a smile that beckoned to his soul.

He shook his head to clear the memory and ran his hands over his rough face, feeling the night's growth of whiskers. He needed to pump water, and build a fire, and make a list of supplies he would need. There was plenty of work to be done and hopefully the physical labor would keep the dark thoughts at bay. And the softer thoughts of Emma Dawson, too.

A few hours later Tyler was washed up and shaved. He had eaten two more of Emma's muffins for breakfast, along with dark, strong coffee made over a fire in the front yard. He had removed most of the plywood from the windows of the cabin, except for the loft, which he couldn't reach without a ladder.

The list of supplies on the small table in the kitchen was growing by the minute. He would need all new window screen for the front porch, and a small bundle of shingles and tar paper for the roof, caulking to seal the chinks in the cabin and around the windows, some wood planking to fix the floor where the roof had leaked, and many more tools than what he had brought with him. He mentally calculated his bank account, thinking this summer of rest was going to cost him a bundle!

The sun was well up in the sky when Tyler drove his pickup slowly through town to the hardware store. He found a spot to park along the curb and climbed out as the familiar dread of facing strangers crept along his spine. With a steadying breath he reached for the door. Why did a picture of Emma Dawson suddenly pop into his mind? The acceptance that had shone in her eyes prodded him forward, encouraging him to step into the next stage of the healing process.

Several older gentlemen crowded the small store, passing the time of day with the man behind the counter. All eyes were drawn to Tyler's tall frame as he opened the plate glass door and stepped inside. A few men nodded a greeting, their eyes falling briefly on the scar across Tyler's face before sliding away. Self-consciousness skittered over him and Tyler fought the urge to turn around and run back out of the store. As the men went back to their conversation, Tyler made his way up and down the aisles, looking for the items on his list.

"So anyways, I tell my wife, it was just a little bit of petty vandalism. Nothing to get all worried about," a man in a John Deere cap said. "But Gloria just got more and more upset. She can't believe that could happen right here in town, during the busy time of year. She keeps saying maybe we should get a dog. She hates dogs!"

"Yeah, my Jenny was all upset when she heard, too, even though we live farther out from town. And then she worried about Emma, seeing as it was her property that was damaged, and her living all alone," the man behind the counter spoke up.

Tyler froze at the mention of Emma's name.

What property had been damaged? Carrying an armload of small tools and plumbing supplies, Tyler walked toward the counter and deposited the items.

"Is there something I can help you with?" the man behind the counter asked.

"Well actually, there probably is." Tyler reached into the back pocket of his jeans and pulled out his list. "I'm staying out at my uncle's cabin for the summer, and it's in pretty sad shape. I need all of these things here for starters."

"Oh, you must be Milt's nephew!" The man smiled in recognition. "Your uncle called here just this morning and said you would probably be stopping in. He said to give you carte blanche, whatever you need. Gave me his credit card number for the bill. 'Bout time somebody did something with that place. How is the old coot anyway?"

"Not bad," Tyler answered slowly. He had better call his uncle right quick. There was no way Uncle Milt could know the extent of the repairs needed on the cabin and the cost. "I'm not sure though, that Uncle Milt knew what he was doing when he said I could buy whatever was needed. There's a lot on that list, including several rolls of window screen and shingles. That's going to add up pretty quick."

"Not to worry. Milt said to take care of it all. He's just happy to have someone working on the old place. Said maybe him and Mabel would come up before the summer is over. It sure would be great to see them again. It's been too long, too long. Don't you think Bill?"

"Yep, it sure would be nice to see the old geezer

again," Bill answered. "You're taking on a big job boy, fixing up that cabin. The place has been disintegrating on its foundation for years." He lifted the bill of his cap and scratched his forehead.

"Well, it certainly is more than I expected when I headed up here," Tyler agreed. "And I hope I don't do all this work for nothing. Did I hear you mention something about some vandalism here in town?" Tyler tried to sound casual though his heart was beating heavily.

"Sure did." Bill was more than glad to fill the stranger in on the latest news. "Happened sometime during the night, just a block over where M33 heads north out of town. You know where Emma Dawson lives in that Victorian house she fixed up, used to be the Nolan place?"

When Tyler shook his head no, Bill continued.

"Of course you wouldn't know, you being new to town. Anyway, seems somebody spray painted her fence, and the stop sign at the corner, and all over the sidewalk. Some sort of message. Threatening Emma, I think, but the sheriff's department is trying to keep a lid on that. They got a crew over there now cleaning it up."

"I'm just glad whoever did it didn't spray paint all over Emma's house," the man from behind the counter said as he moved about the store finding the items on Tyler's list. "She's worked miracles with that old place and it's a real beauty now. The fence is bad enough, but at least that is easily repaired."

"Just makes you wonder what the world is coming to," Bill said sadly. "It surely does. We don't normally have that kind of thing here. Sure, once in awhile some kids will go out to an empty cabin and make mischief, but for the most part people are pretty respectful of other people's property. To think even the street signs right here in town aren't safe!"

But for some reason, the safety of the town's street signs was not foremost in Tyler's mind. All he could think of was a woman with hazel eyes and a blinding smile and a vandal lurking just outside her door.

Over in the Spot of Tea Shop, the air was abuzz with the same conversation. It seemed the night time vandalism was the talk of the town. And with Emma being the victim she had to field everyone's questions, along with their concern and words of advice.

She moved through the morning in a daze. After Nate had taken her to see the graffiti he had called in a work crew to start cleaning it up. He had promised to try and keep the general public from learning the message, but Atlanta was a small town and the people on the work crew would no doubt spread the news.

Emma really didn't want to take it too seriously. Yes, the words were pretty suggestive, but she still figured it was some bored teenager acting on a dare. A slight shiver of apprehension danced over her skin as she remembered the shadow she had seen as she pulled into her driveway last night. She had put it down to the clouds passing over the moon. But had it been? Had someone been lurking out by her garage?

"Emma dear, what are you going to do?" Jeanette Hughes asked anxiously when Emma approached her and her husband, Dan, at their regular corner table by the front windows.

"I don't know that there is much I can do, Jeanette," Emma answered as she set two plates of warm scones on the table and added pots of jam from the tray she carried. "I must trust in the Lord for my protection for 'He only is my rock and my salvation; He is my defense, I shall not be greatly moved,'" she quoted from Psalm 62 as she placed two delicate china cups and saucers in front of the couple and a tea pot full of hot water.

"That's all well and good to trust God, Emma, but maybe you should think about getting a dog, too," Jeanette said as she poured steaming water into her cup and dunked her tea bag up and down. "I mean really, that juvenile spray painted practically right outside your door!" Jeanette picked up a scone and slathered it with raspberry jam, in an obvious state of distress.

"I can't get a dog, I'm here at the shop all day, six days a week." Emma laid a comforting hand on Jeannette's plump shoulder. "Honestly Jeanette, don't get so worked up over this. It's not good for your health, and we don't want the tourists thinking the town is full of trouble and leaving early, do we?" Emma looked pointedly around her little shop, still full with the morning crowd. "They've already got people cleaning up the mess and the sheriff is busy right now trying to find the culprit. We are all perfectly safe."

"I'm sure you're right." Jeanette covered Emma's hand with her own and gave it an affectionate pat.

"We just all worry about you, that's all, living by yourself. And it's scary when this sort of thing happens in a quiet town."

"I know, but we must remember, from whence comes our help? 'My help comes from the Lord, who made heaven and earth.'" With a final squeeze of Jeannett's shoulder, Emma took her large black tray and headed for the kitchen.

"Oh Emma, you and your Bible quotes," Jeanette laughed after her, but her voice no longer held the note of anxiety it had a few moments ago.

Back in the kitchen, Emma took a deep breath and looked at the clock. It was only ten. She had practically an entire day ahead of her to hear nothing but talk of the vandalism, and she was tired of it already.

Yes, she *knew* it had happened right outside her door! Did the locals really think she needed to be constantly reminded of that fact? What would they say if they knew the vandal's intentions, to bring her down a notch or two? She couldn't help the pin pricks of fear that ran up her slender spine. What if someone had broken in while she had been out at the McGillis place?

Take your own advice, Emma chided herself. *Trust in the Lord.* A quiet prayer was all it took for Emma to once more feel the peace that passes all understanding. She picked up her laden tray and headed back to the dinning room, determined to wait on her customers with a confident smile.

Tyler couldn't seem to help himself. After leaving the hardware store with his truck bed full of supplies, he purposely turned and headed north out of town, past Emma Dawson's place, justifying his actions by saying he needed to go to the grocery store.

The house was impossible to miss, sitting back on its deep lot, with its neat white picket fence and gingerbread trim. Two Montmorency County sheriff's cars were parked at the corner, and a work crew was busy repainting the fence, replacing the stop sign and trying to erase the graffiti from the sidewalk. A group of teenagers gawked from the opposite corner

Had the graffiti really held a threatening message for Emma? Tyler glanced over at the gang of teenagers as he drove through the corner and on through town. It was probably just some kid, bored already now that school was out for the summer and looking for some fun and attention. It seemed to him already, in his short experience with Atlanta, that everyone knew everybody else. If someone had it out for Emma, someone else would know. Comforted by that thought, Tyler concentrated on driving on to the grocery store, dispelling thoughts of Emma Dawson and her safety from his mind.

CHAPTER FIVE

At the small grocery store, Tyler bought, along with his groceries, a long distance phone card so he could call his aunt and uncle. After the huge bill he had just rung up at the hardware, there was no way Tyler wanted to add to the expense by calling collect. After unloading his cart of groceries into the back of his pickup, Tyler walked to the edge of the parking lot to the pay phone. Only moments passed before he heard Aunt Mabel's voice on the other end of the line.

"Hey, Aunt Mabel, it's Tyler."

"Ty! Oh, it's so great to hear from you! How is Atlanta and the cabin?" The unmasked affection in his aunt's voice warmed Tyler's heart.

"Well, it's okay. The cabin needs a little more work than Uncle Milt expected." Tyler made a face at the huge understatement. "I'm a little worried about the amount of money it's going to cost."

"Oh don't you worry about that," Mabel

dismissed the thought of financial concerns. "How is town? Did you stop in and say hello to Emma for us?"

"Yeah, yeah I did." Tyler nodded at his end of the phone, wanting to avoid the subject of Emma Dawson. He brushed his blond hair back from his forehead and squinted into the sun. "She's fine. She makes good muffins, that's for sure."

Mabel laughed. "That's for sure. Anything else exciting going on up there?"

"Well, it does seem the town had some excitement last night. A vandal spray painted Emma's fence and some road signs and the sidewalk." Tyler heard Aunt Mabel's quick intake of breath and could have bit off his tongue.

"Emma's fence? Is she okay? Did anything else get damaged?" Distress rang in his aunt's words. "Tyler, you must check on her, make sure she's all right. What would I say to Carolynn if anything happened to their Emma?"

"I'm sure she's fine, Aunt Mabel," Tyler tried to soothe. Why had he brought up the subject? Stupid, stupid, he silently berated himself. "I drove right by her place, nothing happened to the house, just the sidewalk and fence got a little graffiti, that's all. Two cop cars were parked right on the corner just now. There's nothing to be worried about. It was probably just some kid out to get his kicks."

"But you don't know that for sure. Tyler, you have to protect her, she's all alone up there. The poor girl lives by herself. What if someone broke in to her house?"

Protect. The word sent Tyler's mind spinning

back in time to the accident that had taken a young child's life. At one time it had been his job to serve and protect, to help people and save lives, but instead he had taken one. He was in no position to protect Emma or anyone else.

"Aunt Mabel, don't worry. From what I heard at the hardware store, she has more than half the town looking out for her. Now can I talk to Uncle Milt real quick. I want to tell him what I needed for the cabin."

"I'll let you talk to your uncle just as soon as you promise me you'll keep an eye on Emma for us. Honestly Ty, I think it's the least you can do for an elderly aunt and uncle, to help put our minds at ease, considering how far away we live," Mabel used that persuasive tone that Tyler could never resist.

"What's this I hear Mabel, what's wrong with Emma?" Tyler could hear his uncle's voice in the background and Mabel took her mouth away from the phone to answer him.

"There's been some vandalism Milt, right outside Emma's front door. I'm just telling Tyler he has to watch out for her." Mabel spoke into the phone once more. "Promise me Ty, that you'll stop in and see that Emma's okay."

Tyler hesitated. What was he doing, making promises he probably couldn't keep?

"Sure Aunt Mabel, I'll check in on her, but I think you're making a mountain out of a mole hill. It was just a little petty vandalism. I'm sure it has nothing to do with Emma."

"Maybe not, but you can never be sure. It will help this old woman rest easier, knowing we've got you to keep an eye on things. Here's Milt. Goodbye Ty, take care of our Emma now." Mabel handed the phone to her husband, much to Tyler's relief.

"What's going on up there that has your aunt all in a tizzy?"

"Uncle Milt, really, it's nothing to worry about." Tyler purposely evaded the question and changed the subject. "I really called to talk about the cabin. I went to the hardware store and got some of the materials to start the repairs. The owner told me he had talked to you and that all of it was to go on your bill. It's an awful lot Uncle Milt, I think you might want to reconsider." Tyler named the final total, but Milt just shrugged it off.

"Don't worry about it Tyler, I can more than afford it. You don't know what a favor you're doing for me, fixing the place up. Just wish my body wouldn't have betrayed me like this so I could have done the work myself. Matter-of-fact, I wish I could be up there now, helping you. But I know you want to be alone. Do whatever you think is best and buy whatever you need, don't worry about the cost. It's all taken care of."

They talked of the cabin repairs for a few more minutes before Tyler hung up, his hand lingering on the receiver hanging in its silver cradle. His mind was not on the job he was here to do, but on his aunt's command that he should protect Emma. As if he could.

Shaking his head, Tyler headed toward his pickup, thinking that involvement with Emma Dawson was the last thing on earth he needed. He had come up here to get away from it all, escape pressures and well meaning friends and family. He just wanted to hide in the woods and lick his wounds, regain some of the strength he had lost.

As he climbed into the cab of his truck, his eyes fell on the rolls of window screen and stacks of other building materials in the back. His uncle had just paid for all of that. How could he accept Uncle Milt's generosity and not do the one thing his aunt had asked in return, to keep an eye on their friend's daughter? With a heavy sigh of resignation, Tyler pulled out of the parking lot and headed back to the cabin, knowing full well he couldn't.

The afternoon crowd was just beginning to thin out when Emma heard a light knock at the kitchen door of the Spot of Tea. Wiping her hands on her flowered apron, she walked over and looked out the window to see Kirt and Jesse, the two teenagers she had hired to pick wild blueberries for her. With a big smile, she opened the door.

"Hey guys, what have you got for me?" she asked as the two lanky boys crowded in to the shop's kitchen.

"We brought you a good size bucket of blueberries, Miss Dawson." Kirt, the older of the two, handed over a silver minnow bucket with pride.

"We found a big patch of 'em up on Radio Tower Road," Jesse added, blowing his brown hair out of his eyes and hiking up his drooping jean shorts. "Take a look." He nodded toward the bucket Emma held in her hands. She moved over to the counter and unlatched the lid.

"Ooh," she sighed with enthusiasm. "These look great guys." She blessed the two boys with one of her best smiles, making them blush and look down at their feet. "How much do you figure you have here, about four quarts?" The boys just shrugged. "Well, over at the produce market, blueberries are selling for about a dollar fifty a pint, so how about twelve dollars, does that sound fair?"

Kirt and Jesse looked at each other then nodded at Emma, grinning.

Emma went out front to the cash register, returning to hand each boy six dollars. She found a clean colander and emptied the blueberries into it, handing Kirt the minnow bucket.

"Come back again when you have some more. You know I'll buy them from you as long as they're in season." Emma opened the back door to let the boys out, her eyes falling on the two picnic tables situated behind the shop.

The tea shop building had once been an ice cream parlor, with tables outside for the customers. Emma had left two of the octagonal tables out back, painting them light lavender to match the shop. Once in awhile customers would sit outside and eat their muffins and drink their coffee to go. Now Emma noticed a lone young man sitting at one of the tables, staring at the tea shop.

"What's Adam Pearson doing sitting over there?" Emma asked Kirt, pointing with her chin toward the boy with shaggy black hair, wearing jeans with holes in the knees and an expression that could cut through glass.

"Who knows?" Kirt answered, kicking his skate board up from where he had left it leaning against the building.

"Yeah, he's weird," Jesse stated, stuffing his money in his pocket and hopping on his skateboard. "See ya later Miz Dawson."

"Okay, thanks again boys." Emma gave a small wave as the boys headed off down the sidewalk toward town, her expression puzzled as she looked once more toward where Adam Pearson sat alone.

She was still wondering over Adam's presence when she walked back into the dinning room. But when the silver bell tinkled over the front door and Nate Sweeney walked in, Emma forgot about Adam and remembered the event of earlier in the day.

"Hey Emmy, got a minute?" Nate removed his shiny billed hat and brushed a hand through his mahogany hair with its military short cut.

"Sure, Nate." Emma walked around the front counter and out into the nearly empty dinning room. Nate followed her to one of the back tables where they could have a little privacy. "Did you find out anything more?" Emma asked as she sat down, arranging the skirt of her floral sundress.

"No, not so far." Nate set his hat on the table and looked into Emma's eyes. "The crew is finished. Your fence looks good as new. You'll owe the guys a muffin or two." Nate smiled his hundred watt smile, driving away some of Emma's anxiety. "Did you see anything at all? Now that you've had a chance to think about it, did you hear or see anything out of the ordinary?"

"No." Emma shook her head, making her pony-tail sway. "Like I told you, I left home at five this morning. It was still dark, so I didn't even know about the graffiti until you told me. I couldn't even see it when I left the house."

"But what about last night?"

Again Emma shook her dark head. "No, I didn't hear anything unusual. I was out until well after sunset. I got home around 9:45." Suddenly she recalled the flicker of movement she thought she had seen pulling into her drive. Goosebumps formed on her arms and she couldn't repress a shiver. Nate noticed.

"What is it?" he asked, concern showing in his ice blue eyes.

"Nothing really, it's just that, when I pulled into the driveway…" Emma shook her head again, feeling silly, and looked away from the deputy's probing gaze. "It won't be any help to you at all. It's just that, when I pulled into the driveway, I thought I saw something go around the corner of the house. But really, I'm sure it was just a shadow from the trees. I didn't actually *see* anything." Emma didn't want to think that it might have been the vandal lurking around her front door.

"And then after that, what did you do?" Nate continued with his questions.

"I went in and took a shower, then I called my mom and went to bed. I didn't hear a thing all night."

"It could have happened while you were in the shower but most likely they waited until all the lights were out. The town pretty much rolls up the sidewalks by ten and not much traffic goes through. Your bedroom is at the back of the house, so you probably wouldn't have heard anything, especially if you're a really heavy sleeper."

Nate tried to lighten the mood with a wink and a smile, neither of which had any affect on Emma. She was still thinking about someone lurking under her windows while she was in the shower. The words left on her fence suddenly took on a whole new meaning. Nate seemed to read her mind.

"Don't worry your pretty head about it Emmy." He got up from his chair and snagged his hat off the table. "You've got Montmorency County's finest working on the case. We'll have an extra patrol going through town. Just let us know if you see or hear anything out of the ordinary or the least bit suspicious."

"Yes, yes I will," Emma agreed as she, too, rose from her chair. A picture of Adam Pearson sitting alone at the table behind the shop popped into her mind. But could that really be labeled suspicious? Most likely he was just waiting to meet some friends or something. She decided not to mention it to Nate.

"Got big plans for the Fourth of July, Emmy?" Nate asked, a hopeful gleam in his eye as he arranged his hat on his hair.

"I'll be working, of course. Can't close up the shop on the biggest tourist day of the year, now can I?" Emma went behind the counter as Nate headed for the door.

"No, I suppose not. I'll be working crowd

control for the parade, then after that, well, business will be hopping for the sheriff's department, I'm afraid. See you around, Emmy. Remember to call if you see or hear anything."

"I will Nate." Emma waved as the deputy backed out the front door, giving her one last, hope-filled look.

Emma was well aware of Nate's interest in her. In the three years since she had moved back to town, Nate had done everything but stand on his head, trying to catch her attention. He was drop dead gorgeous, held a well respected position in the community and was a strong Christian to boot. Emma considered him a good friend. Why in the world didn't she feel a thing when he directed his hundred watt smile her way?

* * *

Tyler squatted on the roof of the cabin, shirt off, sweating in the hot sun as he hammered tar paper over the hole in the steep roof. With a hefty whack, he sunk the last nail and dropped the hammer. Sitting down wearily, he wiped the drops of sweat off his brow with the back of his hand and squinted up at the sky. What time was it? he wondered. It felt like he had been up on the roof all day.

Picking up his hammer, he made his way carefully down the steep incline to the porch roof and the ladder leaning up against the side of the cabin. Every muscle ached. It was humiliating to find how much stamina he had lost over the last few months, spending so much time in a hospital bed, recovering from surgery after surgery. Even after all the physical therapy, he was as weak as a baby.

His legs felt like wet noodles as Tyler climbed down the ladder. He went in and fetched himself a cold drink, carrying both the bottled water and a dining room chair out onto the porch. Flopping down with a heavy sigh, he looked with disgust at the torn screens. Tomorrow, after the roof was fixed, he would tear all the old screens out and start replacing them. If he could move, that is. A grimace crossed over his face as he raised his scarred arm to take a drink. Yes, he was tired, yes, he was sore, but he *was* getting stronger, he could feel it.

A loud rumble from his stomach reminded Tyler that it had been hours since he had eaten, and his body needed nourishment to keep getting stronger. He got up and went back into the cabin. In the small kitchen area he looked over the food stuffs he had bought. The stove and refrigerator still weren't working. Tyler hadn't had the nerve yet to pull the appliances out and find out how much damage the mice and chipmunks had done to them. The thought of building a fire out front and cooking something wasn't the least bit appealing.

Without warning, a vision of Emma danced across his mind. His mouth watered at the thought of the sandwiches she had fed him last night. Well, he *had* promised Aunt Mabel he would check on her. So what would it hurt if he killed two birds with one stone and satisfied his hunger at the same time?

Tyler set to work pumping cold water into the

chipped enamel sink, washing away the sweat and grime from his day's work. Toweling off with one of Emma's rose pink towels, he walked back to the bedroom and retrieved a clean T-shirt from his duffel bag. He couldn't admit to himself that it was more than physical hunger that drove him into town toward Emma Dawson's restaurant.

CHAPTER SIX

Traffic was light down the main street of town. Tyler turned east and headed the short distance to the Spot of Tea Shop. His heart sank when he saw the parking lot was completely empty and the windows were dark. A bright light shone at the back of the shop. After what he had heard in town, Tyler's instincts were instantly on high alert. He pulled into the lot and parked. As he walked to the plate glass door, he glimpsed Emma working in the kitchen, so he walked around to the back door.

At his light knock, the cake pan Emma held fell to the floor with a loud clatter. She spun around, a hand to her heart. When she saw Tyler's face through the glass, relief lightened her features and she moved to unlock the door.

"Tyler, you about gave me a heart attack," Emma admonished as she let him in.

"Just a bit jumpy, aren't you?" he asked, stepping

into the kitchen with its heavy scent of cinnamon and orange. "I suppose, with that business last night, you have a right to be."

"You heard about that?" Emma bent to retrieve the cake pan. Tyler couldn't help but admire the way her cotton sundress draped over her slender hips and the way her apron ties rode the small of her back.

"Hard not to." Tyler scratched the bridge of his nose with a forefinger and averted his gaze, looking instead at the baked goods lined up on the counter. "It was the talk of the town everywhere I went."

"Tell me about it. If I never have to answer another question, it will be too soon."

"Well, I, um…" He cleared his throat. "I was a little worried when I saw the light on, but no cars, that's why I stopped."

"Oh, I walk here every morning." Emma began stacking wrapped muffins into boxes. "After I close up, sometimes I stay and experiment with new recipes. Here." She reached for a sticky bun cooling on the counter and handed it to Tyler. "I've never made these before, tell me what you think."

Tyler had no choice but to take the gooey confection from her, their hands brushing as he did so. The slight contact seemed to warm him more than the heat coming from the cooling oven. He took a small bite, trying to form a cohesive thought with those hazel eyes looking at him so guilelessly. He chewed slowly and nodded.

"It's good?" Emma asked, a smile breaking over her features. "They're called Chelsea Buns, very English." She resumed packing away the muffins. "I think I'll make several batches when I come in tomorrow."

"What time do you normally come in?" Tyler asked, licking honey from his fingers.

"I get here at five." Emma carried the large boxes out to the front of the store.

"And you don't drive?" Tyler asked slowly, following a few steps behind. He noticed a vinyl zippered bag laying on the counter next to the cash register.

"No. It's silly to drive two blocks, and then take up a parking space. My lot is small enough as it is." Emma set the boxes on the table nearest the door then turned to face him.

Tyler leaned against the end of the counter, crossing his arms over his chest. "And after you close up, you walk home by yourself?"

"Yes." Irritation hung at the edge of the word. "But first I walk to the bank and make my deposit. Then I just cross the street and I'm at my front door. No big deal."

"And pretty much everyone in town knows your routine?"

"Sure, I suppose." Emma waved her hands in frustration. "Really Tyler, I don't know what you're getting at." She moved back toward the kitchen. "I've been doing the same thing for three years."

Tyler refused to budge. "I know you said you were tired of questions about the vandalism, but I have to ask. Was it threatening to you?"

"How did you know?" His question had given her pause.

"Word around town." Tyler shrugged. "So it's true?"

"There was some mention of my virtue. I would like to leave it at that." A pink stain colored her cheeks as she once again moved toward the kitchen.

"Maybe you should think about driving for awhile, until this vandal is caught." Tyler made no move to clear her path. He had promised Aunt Mabel he'd watch out for Emma. He had to make her see that walking to work in the dark of morning and then strolling down the sidewalk with a bag full of money in the evening, was not the safest thing to do, even in her tiny home town. His eyes fell to the vinyl bag next to the cash register.

"Just about everyone knows your routine. The kid who did that vandalism last night probably knows. Suppose he decides to wait for you and snatch that bag of money out of your hand on your way to the bank?"

"That would never happen! Tyler, people here aren't like that. I'm sure that what happened last night was just some teenagers with too much time on their hands. And besides." She moved closer and laid a delicate hand on his arm. The eyes that looked up at him were full of peace. "I trust in the Lord to protect me. The Bible says 'In God I have put my trust; I will not be afraid. What can man do to me?' I won't live in fear, Tyler. Because I have Jesus with me, I don't have to."

A storm began to brew within him and he threw off her hand . Spinning around he stomped back into the kitchen.

"No offense Emma, but that's just stupid. God isn't running around playing bodyguard for all the humans on earth. You're fooling yourself if you think He cares for one minute what happens to you." Tyler stood at the back door staring out, his body rigid. He felt Emma's quiet presence behind him. Some invisible force made Tyler turn around and he fought the pull that seemed to drag his gaze to hers.

"It may seem stupid to you, but I know in my heart that God does care about me. He cares about you, too. He is watching out for us every minute. The Bible says that not a sparrow falls from the sky but that God sees it."

Tyler snorted in disbelief.

"Yeah, well, if God cared so much, if He loved everyone so much, then He wouldn't..." his voice trailed off and he looked away. "Forget it."

"Then He wouldn't let accidents happen? Is that what you were going to say?" Emma took another step closer and Tyler found he could no longer avoid looking into those hazel eyes that beckoned to him. He saw the understanding there, the compassion, and most puzzling, the peace. He finally nodded, one slow nod of his head.

"Yeah, that's what I was going to say."

"I don't know why God lets accidents happen. But I do know that all things work together for good for those that love Jesus. Even bad things. Even accidents can be used for good and God's glory."

Tyler remained skeptical. Emma gave one of her small shrugs and turned away.

"I'm nearly done here." She motioned toward the

kitchen counter. "Since you are so worried about my safety, can I get you to drive me to the bank and then home?" Emma began covering the sticky buns with heavy plastic wrap. She glanced up at the clock. "Sheesh, seven-thirty. No wonder I'm starving. Did you eat dinner yet?"

"Actually, no." Tyler shook his head, remembering that hunger is what had driven him to Emma's in the first place. "That's what I was doing in town, I came to get a bite to eat."

"It's a beautiful evening," Emma commented as she put things away with deft efficiency. "I could whip us up some sandwiches and we could eat at the township park. I've got tons of stuff here. Do you like chicken salad? Or egg salad? I could make you watercress, but I doubt that would fill you up." Emma looked him up and down from behind the refrigerator door and smiled. Tyler couldn't stop the corner of his mouth lifting in answer, their disagreement of a moment ago forgotten in the bright force of her girlish grin.

"Okay, sure, sandwiches in exchange for your safe passage back home," Tyler agreed and was once more rewarded with a smile that made his heart lift.

Briley township park on the banks of the Thunder Bay River was a quiet oasis in the center of town. Several people cast their fishing lines into the water from the low dam at the far end while a mother pushed two small children on the swings. Emma carried a sack with their dinner, Tyler following behind with two large foam cups of iced tea. She led them to a picnic table near the water's edge.

With a contented sigh, Emma sat down and began dividing the food between them. This time Tyler was not surprised when Emma bowed her head and said a brief prayer, although his eyes opened wider when she included the vandal in her petitions. After she said "amen" Tyler quirked an eyebrow at her, but said nothing. Instead he took a huge bite out of his sandwich.

"This is the best bread," he finally said once he had swallowed.

"I get it from the Elk Horn bakery," Emma explained. "We have a barter system, muffins for bread. That's one of the things I was doing when you showed up, getting their order ready for tomorrow. I think when I opened up, people expected a rivalry between me and the Elk Horn, but there never has been. We've worked out a deal that's mutually bene-ficial and we respect the niche we both have in the community. I don't try to sell pie, and they don't sell watercress sandwiches." Emma smiled and winked as she bit into a celery stick. Tyler felt an electric current sear through him. He watched in fascination as she took a long drink of iced tea.

"So, what did you do on the cabin today?"

"I worked on the roof mostly." Tyler forced his eyes away from the pink tongue that licked drops of tea from her lips. He took a sip of his own cold drink, trying to quench the flare of longing that Emma had unknowingly ignited.

"I got the plywood off the windows, took all that garbage to the landfill, then came into town and got a truck load of materials. Found out that Uncle Milt had already called the hardware and made arrangements for me to get whatever was needed. I felt guilty, because it came to a *whole* lot, but when I called, he said not to worry about it." Tyler shrugged, thinking about what else had been said during that phone call. His promise to Aunt Mabel to keep an eye on Emma.

"I'm sure Milt is thrilled to have you working on the place," Emma reassured him. "It used to be such fun, visiting there. I grew up right next door, you know." The look Tyler shot her told her that he hadn't. "The next driveway down, that was my parent's place. We had the greatest time living there on the lake. There were always so many people in and out all summer. And Milt and Mabel would come up and spend the summer at their cabin. Of course, they were a lot younger then. But Mabel was always so much fun. It was like a giant adventure to her."

"Your parents, they don't live up here any more?" Tyler asked as he balled up the wrappings from his sandwich. Emma shook her head sadly.

"No, they sold out about four years ago. I had gone off to college, graduated and was working downstate. Then Milt had his first heart attack and they stopped coming up. It seemed all the people we had known when I was growing up, they all aged. Their kids grew up and got scattered and everyone stopped coming for the summer. Mom was lonely and dad was tired of spending six months of the year snowed in, so they sold and moved down to Toledo to be near Milt and Mabel. To hear them talk, you would think they moved to Florida. The winters are so mild down there," Emma mimicked with a grin.

"What made you move back then?" Tyler found he was actually interested, actually enjoying having a conversation. He was amazed to find he was no longer plagued by the self consciousness that had kept him chained for the last three months.

He leaned an elbow on the table, resting his face in his hand. Absently his finger ran over the ridge of scar on his cheek, but the old ghosts didn't rush in to haunt him. His eyes rested on the woman sitting across from him. Wisps of dark hair had escaped her ponytail and had curled softly in the heat, framing her heart shaped face.

"Oh, I always wanted to come back. To me, this is home. I always missed it. Then a few years ago my grandmother died and left me a small inheritance. When I had come home to help my mom pack, after they sold their place, I had seen the old Dairy Freeze building was for sale and I could just picture it as a tea room. The money from my grandmother made it possible for me to buy the building, and the house. I know I'm blessed. I didn't have to fight and claw to make my dream come true, but I do work hard now. Which reminds me." She glanced down at her wrist watch. "I'd better be getting home. My day starts very early."

As Emma rose from the picnic table, her eye was drawn to something up the hill. She hesitated and seemed to pale slightly. Tyler looked up with a worried frown.

"What is it?" he asked. Concerned, he looked

over his shoulder following Emma's line of vision. A dark haired boy in tattered jeans straightened away from the tree and sauntered away down the path. Emma shook herself.

"Nothing, it's nothing, it's just, that boy." She shook her head and moved away from the picnic table, up the hill toward the parking lot.

"What about that boy, Em?" He was still puzzled as he followed her to the truck.

"Nothing." She smiled at him over her shoulder as she climbed in his pickup. "He just needs a lot of prayer, that's all."

Emma's phone was ringing when she came out of the steaming bathroom, her head wrapped in a thick, yellow towel. She plopped down on the coverlet of her bed and snatched up the receiver.

"Hello." With one hand holding the phone, Emma used her other hand to unwind the towel and began rubbing it over her wet hair.

"Emma, it's Mom. Is everything okay up there?" At her mother's worried tone Emma's hand stilled and she dropped the damp towel onto her lap.

"What do you mean, Mom? Why wouldn't everything be okay?"

"Well, I talked to Mabel and she said there had been some vandalism to your house. I waited all day for you to call and tell me what happened, then I finally decided I'd call you." Her mother sounded slightly put out.

"How in the world did Mabel find out about the vandalism?" Emma asked, knowing the answer before her mother could reply. Tyler had said he had talked to his uncle earlier today.

"She talked to that nephew of hers. Now Emma, tell me what happened," her mother commanded. "I want to hear all the details."

"Honestly Mother, there's not much to tell." Emma sighed. Never had obviously arrived. "Somebody spray painted my fence and the sidewalk and the street signs right here at the corner. That's all I know. It's no big deal." Determined to keep it light, Emma decided she *would not* tell her mother what the graffiti had said. "The way people have talked you would think no one has ever vandalized anything in Atlanta before."

"Well, it is a little slow in the excitement department. And you can't be too careful nowadays. You have such a beautiful house and lovely things. You wouldn't want someone stealing anything, or, heaven forbid, hurting you."

Did her mother already know what the message had said? No, she couldn't possibly, because Tyler didn't know.

"I don't think you have to worry about anything like that happening, Mom," Emma tried to reassure. "And you'll be happy to know, Nate Sweeney is on the case." Emma couldn't help but smile into the phone. Her mother snorted.

"Heaven help you! Nate Sweeney. That does not give me any peace of mind. That boy is more interested in primping in the mirror than catching criminals."

"Mother!" Emma felt she should jump to Nate's

defense. "Is that any way to talk about an officer of the law?"

"Oh pish-posh, you know it's true," Carolynn continued. "And as your mother I'm entitled to worry. I've been calling since seven. Where have you been?"

"I stayed after work to try out a new recipe. Then Tyler stopped by so I made us some sandwiches and we went to the park to eat."

A heavy silence hung suspended over the phone line.

"Emma darling, I don't want to interfere but…"

"Then don't," Emma cut off her mother's words.

"Okay, but you will be careful, won't you, I mean about this vandalism business?"

"Oh, honestly, it's not that big of a deal. I don't understand why everyone has become so unhinged just because some teenager sprayed a little paint," Emma said, feeling peeved once more with her mother. "I'm not the least bit worried. I think everyone is blowing this thing way out of proportion." The way her mother was doing with Tyler. Emma didn't like it one bit.

"Well, if you say so." Emma could tell she had hurt her mother's feelings.

"I'm sorry, Mom. I didn't mean to snap at you. It's been a long day."

"I love you, Emma, it's a mother's job to worry."

"You don't have to worry. Everything is perfectly fine."

"I hope so," Carolynn didn't sound convinced.

"Mom, can I ask you a question?" Emma didn't wait for her mother to respond. "Do you remember the Pearsons?"

"The Pearsons? Hmm. Oh yes, she was the poor woman who's husband ran off years ago. Is that who you mean? What was her name?"

"Doreen."

"Oh yes, that's it. Doreen."

"She has a son, Adam."

"Right, I remember now. He was a real handful, poor thing. Why do you ask about them? They aren't the kind of people we usually associate with."

No, they certainly weren't. Emma felt a stab of conscience at the fact. Just the thought of Adam's cold stare gave her a bad case of the shivers.

"Why would you ask about the Pearsons?"

"I don't know, I've just been thinking about them lately, that's all." The twist of truth slipped out easily. "It seems they've had it rough."

"There you go with that tender heart of yours again." Carolynn's smile came across the miles of phone wire. "You can't rescue every lost kitten out there. Remember that, okay?"

"I'll try," Emma agreed.

"Okay, dear. Well, I'll let you get some rest. Call us if you need anything, anything at all."

"I will. Kiss Daddy for me. Goodnight." Hanging up the phone, Emma rose from the bed and padded back to the bathroom, her thoughts a tangled web. Tyler. Adam. Were they both a couple of lost souls that needed saving?

CHAPTER SEVEN

Rain was spattering against Emma's bedroom window when she turned off her alarm at four-thirty the next morning. Well, she thought, dressing in pink jeans and white short sleeved sweater, that took care of one problem. She would have to drive to work in this weather.

But when she dashed through the rain to her car she noticed it seemed to be canted at an odd angle. Bending down she peered through the dark and rain. A flat tire! She walked closer and looked again. Not just one flat tire, two! How in the world? Emma looked toward town. The service station wasn't open at this time of morning and she only had one spare tire. Pulling the hood of her rain coat closer around her face, she bent into the wind and walked toward the tea shop.

On the dot of seven she called Ernie at the service station and explained her dilemma. Not to worry, Ernie reassured her, he'd send someone over to have a look.

The inclement weather kept most people indoors and so the Spot of Tea remained mostly deserted. Wind lashed rain against the large front windows as Emma mixed up batches of Chelsea buns and blueberry muffins. Despite the storm that was raging outside, she felt safe and secure in her snug shop.

When the bell tinkled out front, Emma wiped her hands on her apron and headed to the dining room. Finally, a customer! She smiled when she saw Nate Sweeney shaking droplets of rain from his slicker.

"Hey Nate, needing a cup of coffee to chase the chill away?" Emma asked.

Nate cleared his throat. Remembering his manners, he reached a hand to remove his wet hat from his head.

"No, no thanks Emmy. I'm sorry to say I'm here strictly on business." Nate glanced around the room. "Anyone else here?"

"No, just me and you," Emma answered, puzzled. "Has something else happened?"

"I'm afraid so. I got a call from Ernie at the Amoco this morning. He told me about your tires."

"Yeah, isn't that weird? Two flats at the same time. But I don't see why that calls for police involvement." Emma smiled. "I know things can be pretty slow around here but I didn't know you guys were doing roadside assistance now, too."

Nate's usual flirting smile was strangely absent.

"Your tires were slashed, Emmy. That's why Ernie called me. Someone slashed them. And." He cleared his throat, appearing uncomfortable with the news he had to impart. "There was a note on your seat."

"What did it say?" Emma asked slowly, not sure she wanted to know.

"It said, 'You're goin' nowhere fast but soon I'll give you a ride you'll never forget.'" Nate quoted from memory.

"What exactly is that supposed to mean?" Emma's brows drew together as she frowned.

"It could be taken a couple of ways, neither of them very nice. Someone seems to think you need some excitement in your life. I don't suppose you heard anything last night?"

"I didn't hear a thing, except the thunder that rolled in around midnight. I thought you were supposed to have extra patrols going through town." Emma looked accusingly at Nate.

"We did have an extra patrol going through, but he only made the sweep through town twice between eleven last night and five this morning. The campgrounds are full to overflowing. The sheriff's department is being kept pretty busy. And knifing a couple of tires takes less than a minute." Nate set his hat back on his head, preparing to leave.

"We'll post a stakeout at the corner tonight. Hopefully we'll catch the creep that's doing this." Nate shook his handsome head, frowning. "As if we don't have enough work to do, keeping the Fourth of July crowd from killing themselves with fireworks or killing other people on the road with their drinking and driving. Man, I hate this time of year."

He turned toward the front door. As if feeling her eyes upon him, he turned, his back against the glass.

"It's gonna be okay Emma, I promise." Nate stepped forward and laid strong brown hands on her shoulders. "We'll catch whoever's doing this. You have my word."

"Thanks Nate." Emma forced a smile. "I'll be praying for you. And whoever's doing this, too." Nate nodded and she watched as he pushed open the door and jogged to his cruiser sitting in the rain.

Business was slow throughout the morning and for once Emma was thankful for the lull. Tomorrow was Saturday, her busiest day of the week, and the bad weather gave her a chance to prepare for the bigger crowd she could expect tomorrow, if the weather broke. Unfortunately, it also gave her more time to think over this latest vandalism.

Rhonda came in at nine, as usual, and the small smattering of customers in the dining room was easy enough for her to handle. Emma was more than happy to stay in the kitchen, avoiding as many questions as possible. How long would it be, Emma wondered, before the whole town knew her tires had been slashed? And the note? Who all knew what it said? Ernie for sure. He probably showed it to Blake, who worked for him. It might have even been Blake who found it. Blake Dalton was not likely to keep his mouth shut.

She was the target of someone. The thought left her mouth suddenly dry. But who? Unbidden, a picture of Adam Pearson staring at her flashed into Emma's mind, sending a cold shiver up her spine. Was it Adam? Emma searched her mind for what little information she knew about the family. It wasn't much. Her mother was right, Adam had always seemed to be a handful for his mother, but was he destructive? Emma didn't know the teenager well enough to make any judgements.

Sighing, Emma rubbed her temples, trying to shake the pensive mood that had engulfed her. She walked to the front of the shop as Rhonda was serving coffee and muffins to Jim Deland and his wife, Kay.

"Hey, Emma." Jim motioned to her with a work roughened hand. "What's this I hear about your tires being slashed?" Jim's voice carried throughout the small dining room and all eyes turned his way.

"I had a couple flat tires this morning. Who said they were slashed?" Emma tried to keep her voice even. The cat was definitely out of the bag. She made her way over to the Deland's table.

"Stopped to fill up with gas this morning. Ernie said your tires were slit clear through. Said he called the sheriff. Must make you awfully nervous, having your place vandalized two nights in a row."

"Well, Nate's taking care of it. I'm not worried. Anything else I can get you?"

"I hear someone's fixing up the old McGillis cabin." Jim continued, oblivious to Emma's discomfort. She was reminded of the worst part of living in a small town; everyone knew everyone else's business.

"Yes, that's right. Milt and Mabel's nephew is staying up here for the summer. He's doing a lot of work to the place."

"Seems kinda funny, don't it?" Jim blew across the top of his coffee before taking a small sip. "This guy comes up here and suddenly we have a rash a vandalism in town."

Emma's gaze turned hard.

"Jim Deland, I can not believe you said such a thing," she reprimanded. "Milt and Mabel are my parents oldest and dearest friends. I've met their nephew and he's a very nice man. He's..." Emma hesitated, unsure of how to continue without giving any personal information that would just increase the gossip in town.

"He's here as a favor to Milt, working on that cabin so Milt and Mabel can start using it again," she continued, knowing she was washing the truth in shades of gray. "He's a grown man, not some delinquent teenager. It's crazy that you would even associate Tyler with what has happened here in town!" In her vehement defense, Emma's voice had risen, leaving the entire conversation open to the ears of all the customers.

Looking around, Emma realized what a spectacle she had created. Rhonda stood staring at her, open mouthed. Emma knew she had added more fuel to the gossip that was sure to rampage through Atlanta. Now everyone would want to know just what exactly Tyler McGillis meant to Emma Dawson that she was so fired up in his defense.

"Still, it seems awful co-incidental," Jim drew out the word, sitting back in his chair unfazed. "This guy takes up residence out there on Ryan Road and suddenly we have spray paint and graffiti and slashed tires. And you seem to be the target, Emma." He gave her a knowing look up and down. "I won't be the first person to put two and two together and come up with four. I bet Nate Sweeney will be doing the math himself." With a smirk, Jim went back to his coffee, leaving Emma to return to her kitchen in frustration and fear.

What if Nate did accuse Tyler? Emma clearly saw haunted green eyes. False allegations of vandalism would do nothing to bring about the healing Tyler so desperately needed.

But it had begun after Tyler arrived, a deceptive voice seemed to whisper in her ear. Messed up in the head, her mother had said so. Seeds of doubt fought to take root in her fertile imagination.

No, no, no! Emma shoved the suspicion away. She could not equate Tyler, the hurting man she had met, with a vandal who was set on destroying her property, she didn't care what anyone else might say. Besides, hadn't Tyler been the one to encourage her to drive to work? He wouldn't do that and then slash her tires.

Emma closed her eyes and began to pray.

Lord, You know Tyler did not do this. You know the scars he carries on his body and on his heart. Protect him from these accusations. I don't know what he would do if he thought people were blaming him for what's happened. He came here to find peace, not tribulation. Help Nate find who really is doing this, before Tyler gets hurt. Please God.

Opening her eyes, Emma looked out the back door of the kitchen, unseeing. She had to remember who was in control here. God was in control and He wouldn't give any of them more than they could handle.

Feeling more at peace, her eyes began to focus and she was able to see the rain that continued to fall beyond the kitchen door. And she saw something else, a rain ponchoed figure watching the building from the tree line out back.

Normally, when Emma returned to her house at the end of the day, she felt solace. Like the arms of the old Victorian home embraced her. It was where she could relax and unwind. A place she was proud of and felt blessed to call home. Now, as she drove slowly through the rain on her brand new tires, Emma felt nothing but trepidation and confusion. How could so much have changed in a few short days?

Parking in the driveway, Emma dashed through the rain to the protection of the wide front porch. She unlocked the door and dropped the keys on the pie table in the entryway, stopping to listen for unfamiliar noises. What was happening to her? She shouldn't be feeling this fear in her own home.

"For God has not given us a spirit of fear, but of power and of love and of a sound mind," Emma spoke the words from Second Timothy aloud as she moved through the house to the kitchen, determination in every step.

The phone in the sheriff's office was answered on the first ring.

"Yes, this is Emma Dawson, may I speak to Deputy Sweeney please?"

"Of course Miss Dawson, just a moment please." In no time at all, Nate was on the line.

"Emma, is anything wrong?"

"No, nothing's wrong Nate," Emma reassured. Was that a lie? Suddenly it seemed as if *everything* was wrong. Her world had been turned upside down. "I just need to talk to you about, you know, the vandalism. Can you come by do you think? I'm at home."

"Sure, Emmy, sure. I'll be right there."

Emma was waiting on the front porch when Nate pulled his cruiser up to the curb. Long strides carried Nate up the walk to stand in front of Emma, water dripping from the brim of his hat.

"Come on in, Nate." Emma rose from the settee and opened the front door. Nate removed his rain slicker, draping it over a patio chair before following Emma into her kitchen. She poured him a glass of lemonade and sat at the kitchen table, motioning Nate to do the same.

"I need to ask you a question and I need you to be as honest with me as you can be, under the circumstances." Emma's eyes were solemn as they met Nate's across the table.

"You know that Milt and Mabel McGillis' nephew has come up to fix up their old cabin?" Nate nodded in answer. "Well, someone in the shop today said something that really disturbed me, and I wanted to ask you if it's true or not. This person said that because Tyler came up here at the same time the vandalism started, that he would be a suspect. Is that true?"

Nate sat back in his chair and let out a long sigh.

"It's an ongoing investigation, Emmy. I'm not at liberty to discuss suspects with you. I think you know that."

"But it's absurd to think that Tyler is responsible for what's happened." Emma bit her lip and forged ahead. "I was out at the McGillis cabin the night the vandal did the spray painting. I went out to help Tyler clean up the place, and I stayed until dark. I told you I saw something when I came home, that something went around the side of the house when I pulled in the driveway. It couldn't have been Tyler, I had just left him at the cabin. There's no way he could have gotten into town before I did."

"Emma, you told me that you didn't know what you saw that night," Nate ruthlessly reminded her. "You told me it was probably nothing, just shadows from the trees. It might not have been, most likely wasn't, the vandal. The person who did the graffiti could have done it at any time after you got home. You said you took a shower between nine-thirty and ten. That's plenty of time to drive from Ryan Road."

Emma looked at him in disbelief. "So you're saying that Tyler *is* a suspect? Nate I can't believe this. It's Milt and Mabel's nephew for goodness sake. He's here to recover from an accident! He himself is worried about my safety. He's the one who urged me to drive to work. Why would he do that then slash my tires? That doesn't make any sense!"

"How well do you know this guy, Emma?" Nate's blue eyes bored into hers. "You've known him what, a few days? You've known me all your life. You're going to have to trust me on this. The case is under investigation," he stressed. "At this point we aren't ruling anyone out. If this guy Tyler," Nate said the name with clear distaste. "If he is innocent, then he has nothing to worry about."

Emma squirmed under Nate's intense gaze. Three people now, three people she knew and trusted doubted Tyler. Could there be any grain of truth in their suspicions? Emma rebelled against the idea.

"But what if, what if I had other evidence?"

"What other evidence?" Nate asked slowly, waiting.

Emma looked into her glass of lemonade, picturing Adam Pearson watching her. But had that been Adam this afternoon? The rain poncho made it impossible to tell. Was that evidence? Could she, in good conscience, accuse Adam when all she had to go on was that she had seen him watching her? She had seen him twice yesterday, but in a town as small as Atlanta, seeing a person more than once in a day wasn't unusual. If she mentioned that to Nate, he would think she was merely defending Tyler. Emma shook her head. She wouldn't point a finger at a possibly innocent person, even if it would take the suspicion off Tyler.

"I didn't say I *had* any other evidence," she finally answered. "I just asked what would happen if I *did*."

Nate leaned across the small table and took Emma's hands, looking deep into her eyes.

"Emma please, leave this to me, to the sheriff's office. Don't go sticking your nose into things and putting yourself in more danger. I remember how you used to read all those mysteries when we were teenagers. But this isn't a book. The department is taking these two messages seriously, until we have reason to do otherwise. It could just be a prank, a teenager getting his kicks. But destruction of personal property is serious business. The investigation is open, we aren't ruling anyone out."

He gave her hands a squeeze and got up, pushing his chair under the table. Emma rose too, feeling as if she had failed Tyler.

"Call me whenever you need to Emma, you know I'm always here for you," Nate said. "If you do have any evidence, let me know, but please don't go trying to solve this crime yourself, you'll only get hurt."

But it was obvious by the determined tilt of her chin that Emma Dawson had no intention of staying out of things.

CHAPTER EIGHT

Saturday dawned bright and clear. Emma was thankful to find all her property intact. The unmarked car sitting in the vacant lot behind the pizza parlor must have discouraged the vandal from showing himself for a third night in a row. Emma prayed the excitement was over for good.

The perfect weekend weather meant the tea shop was standing room only the entire day, and when Emma locked the doors at seven o'clock, it was all she could do to drag herself to her car and drive to the bank and home. Most of her weekend business was vacationers, so she had been spared a day of gossip and questions concerning Tyler McGillis and the mystery surrounding the vandalism.

Tyler. How had he kept himself busy the past two days? Had Nate Sweeney been out to question him? Emma prayed not. But would Nate think the vandal hadn't hit last night because Emma had warned Tyler? Would a peaceful night point to Tyler's guilt?

Oh, Lord, this was all so messed up.

Emma passed a weary hand over her eyes. Tomorrow was Sunday. A blissful day of rest, and boy did she need it. The Fourth of July was only a week away, the busiest day of the year for the town. There would be a parade, a beauty contest, canoe races on the Thunder Bay, a picnic and fireworks. Emma took Sundays off, her day of rest, but starting Monday she would be working twice as hard preparing for the crush of people who would pack Atlanta for the holiday. She would need all of her energy for that. She couldn't let Tyler McGillis or the town vandal distract her from the business at hand.

The county police cruiser parked in front of her house made Emma's tired body sit up in alarm. She pulled into her drive and walked up to Nate Sweeney who sat on the porch.

"Nate, anything wrong?"

"Nope, not a thing." Nate rose slowly from the settee and stood back as Emma unlocked her front door. "Town's been perfectly normal for a summer Saturday, I'm glad to say."

"Praise the Lord!" Emma opened the door and entered the cool interior of the house. Nate followed. "So what can I do for you?"

"Actually, I was wondering if you had been out to the McGillis place recently." Nate removed his hat and looked directly into Emma's eyes.

"No." Emma met his gaze four square. "I spent all day today busting my fanny at the shop. Why? Have you been out there to question Tyler?"

Nate shrugged a uniform covered shoulder.

"No, not yet. No reason to at this point. It just seemed a little odd to me, that's all. After our conversation yesterday evening, there wasn't any damage done in town last night. Wondered if you might know why."

"I don't like the implication in your tone, Nate Sweeney," Emma's voice took on an unusual edge. "I haven't spoken to Tyler since Thursday evening. Considering I'm the victim here, I have no reason to meddle in your investigation."

"I know, I know." Nate became contrite. "I'm sorry. I wasn't accusing you of anything." He looked up at the ceiling as if searching the white plaster for answers. Not seeming to find any, he sighed.

"Look, I have a favor to ask. We staked out over there in the empty lot." Nate motioned out the large picture window to the overgrow lot kitty-corner from Emma's yard. "But we don't want to do that again tonight, in case the perpetrator is on to us. I wanted to ask if we could place an officer here in the house with you tonight. A female officer," Nate added, seeing the suspicious look Emma threw his way.

"I suppose so," Emma agreed reluctantly. "You don't think maybe this whole thing is over with? Maybe the vandal got his thrills and won't be doing it anymore."

"I hope so, Emma. But since you've been the target, I think it's prudent to keep our vigilance up for awhile longer. These kinds of people, they don't usually stop once they start and find out they enjoy the excitement."

Emma's heart sank. The vandal most likely

would hit again? She had hoped that the night of tranquility signaled a return to normal. Nate's words dashed those hopes to smithereens.

"Okay somebody can stay here." At least she would feel a little safer, having the law in her living room. And maybe they would catch whoever was doing this.

Two days. Tyler hadn't laid eyes on Emma Dawson in two days. Why then could he still see her, moving across his mind's eye like the soft white clouds that moved quietly across the blue Michigan sky? They had shared two meals together, that was all. So why had the last six meals he had eaten alone all tasted like sawdust? Worse than the hospital food he had lived on for a month.

With a sigh, Tyler rose from the table, leaving his half empty plate to pace around the confines of the cabin. The stormy weather of the day before had kept him indoors, forcing him to finally pull the stove and refrigerator away from the wall and see if they were salvageable. With a little minor repair and some elbow grease, the stove had come to life. But the refrigerator was a lost cause. He would either have to buy another one, or spend time and money running to town every day for ice. He stood at the ladder to the loft and looked up. At least the patch on the roof had held up to the deluge. How had Emma fared?

The question came unbidden to his mind. Had she driven to work as he had asked her to? With the rain yesterday, he supposed she had. Tyler pictured her there in the kitchen of her tea shop, holding out a sticky bun and his chest tightened. She was getting to him. Emma Dawson was cutting right through the scar tissue that had grown over his heart and was making him itch. He rubbed a hand over his face, feeling the deep scar there. He ran a finger down its length, reminded that a woman like Emma Dawson deserved better than a mutilated man, a child killer.

She was perfect, soft, beautiful. Was she also the target of a criminal? Tyler heard his aunt's voice, demanding he promise to keep an eye on Emma. He had to drive into town for ice anyway. What would it hurt to swing by her place and make sure she was okay?

The road to town was covered in no time. Tyler stopped at the blinking red light on Main Street and then proceeded slowly through the intersection, ready to stop at Emma's driveway. The Montmorency County Sheriff's car sitting at her curb gave him pause. On the porch was a tall, dark haired deputy holding his hat against his thigh and smiling down at Emma who lounged in the doorway looking up at him.

Tyler's throat tightened and he clutched the steering wheel, speeding up a little and passing through to the grocery. Yes, that was the kind of man Emma Dawson deserved. Good looking, whole. Someone who really could protect her from the bad guys of this world.

Deputy Lydia Ebersol had worked for the county sheriff for twenty years. At forty-five, she was short and slightly plump with graying ash blond hair in a pixie cut. Emma had known her for a lifetime. She remembered well the many lectures in junior high and high school that Lydia presented on the dangers of drugs and alcohol, drinking and driving, and drag racing around blind curves on the many unpaved roads throughout the county. She felt totally at ease having Lydia take up residence on the overstuffed sofa in the living room.

She was also relieved when Lydia left Sunday morning as Emma got ready for church without making one arrest or having to call in the cavalry. Another quiet night in Atlanta. Perhaps Nate was wrong and things were going to return to normal. Emma was convinced that the two nights of vandalism were merely some bored kids who had gotten a couple of thrills at her expense, nothing more. They'd probably moved on to bigger, more exciting things by now.

With a light heart she drove to church and sat in her familiar pew. The pastor's sermon was based on James 1:2-3, "My brethren, count it all joy when you fall into various trials, knowing that the testing of your faith produces patience."

How perfect. A word in due season. Emma felt God's comforting presence and when they stood to sing how the battle belongs to the Lord, Emma's voice joined in strong and clear. She needed the reminder that the Lord was in control of everything. She had nothing to fear from any foe, vandal or otherwise. Emma left the church feeling like her world was once more set right.

In no hurry to get home, Emma drove slowly down sandy back roads headed toward town. The sky was crystal clear, so blue the intensity almost hurt her eyes. The towering pines lifted their branches heavenward and perfumed the air with their spicy scent. She smiled as she stopped her car so a flock of wild turkeys could cross the road. They disappeared into the thick brush on the other side. Life, she was reminded, was good.

As she leisurely drove home, Emma spotted a bright orange yard sale sign. Sitting in the middle of the gravel driveway was a tan love seat and matching recliner. Emma pulled in, thinking of Tyler and the lack of useable furniture at the cabin. She doubted he had taken the time to look for anything new. Parking, Emma got out of her car and walked over to examine the furniture. It was covered in brushed velour and looked in good shape.

A young woman with a toddler clinging to her hip came out of the blue mobile home and approached Emma.

"Hi, are you interested in the furniture?" Emma looked into tired gray eyes and smiled. The toddler reached out a hand and Emma couldn't resist poking a finger into the baby's belly.

"Yes, I am. It looks like it would be just right for a summer place my friend has up here. What are you asking for it?"

The low figure the woman quoted had Emma reaching into her purse for her check book.

"Can I ask you to hold it for a little while? My friend's cabin isn't far from here and he has a truck. We could be back in less than an hour to get it. Would that be okay?"

The woman readily agreed and Emma went about looking over the rest of the sale, picking up a few other small items she thought Tyler could use. After writing her check, she toted a tea kettle, iron skillet and an outdoor print to her car, assuring the young mother that she would be back shortly for the furniture before driving off toward the McGillis place.

Tyler was on the front porch, ruthlessly tearing down the ragged screening when he saw Emma's blue sedan pull into the driveway. She pulled the car halfway into the overgrown front yard before turning off the ignition. She sat for a moment, watching as Tyler reached up to rip another section of screen away from the wood frame of the porch. Across the expanse of weeds and wildflowers their eyes met and held, then Tyler lowered his arms and slowly turned to retrieve his T-shirt.

His head was just emerging from the collar of his shirt when Emma came walking through the tall grass in a soft yellow dress with a white sailor collar. Oh yes, Sunday, she had just been to church. Her hair was down, flowing dark and thick around her shoulders, enticing Tyler with its long, luxuriant waves. He steeled himself against his reaction to her.

She stopped on the other side of the porch, looking through the now empty hole to where Tyler stood. He couldn't help but notice how the yellow of her dress brought out the golden glints in her hazel eyes. He almost smiled. But then he remembered a tall, dark policeman standing on Emma's porch and the smile died before it could turn up a corner of his lips.

"Well, you've been awfully busy I see," Emma said with a sly smile. She gave him a secretive look out of the corner of her eye, making his heart miss several beats. Tyler's gaze remained cool, not betraying his inner turmoil.

"Yep." Tyler resumed taking down the old screen. He forced the picture of Emma and the good looking cop into his mind, reminding himself that was the kind of man she deserved.

"I have a surprise for you."

The excitement in her voice piqued his curiosity and he couldn't keep his gaze from settling on her. He cocked an eyebrow in question.

"Have you been able to buy any furniture yet?" At the negative shake of his head her smile grew. "Well, I was on the way home from church and I passed a yard sale. I hope you don't mind but I took the liberty of buying you a love seat and recliner. You won't believe it Tyler but I got both pieces for fifty dollars! They'll go perfect in the cabin, they're just the right size. I could just picture them in front of the fireplace. I told the woman we would be back within the hour to get them in your truck. Is that okay?"

Puzzled, Emma picked her way around to the door and entered the porch, stopping in front of Tyler. He forced a coldness into his gaze as she looked up at him. As if transforming before his eyes, Tyler saw the happiness fade out of her face and her good mood disappear.

"I'm sorry, I didn't think," she apologized. "I can go back and tell the woman that you don't want it." Emma looked away through the empty windows to the trees. "Maybe I can think of someone else who could use it."

Her forlorn expression wrenched Tyler's heart. When her smile had disappeared it was if the sun had disappeared behind a cloud. Tyler mentally gave himself a hard shake. The woman before him had a good heart. She had done something thoughtful for him and he stood here like a clod making her sweat in her pretty Sunday dress, all because of his feelings of inadequacy.

"No, that's okay," he finally spoke. "I can use some furniture in there. Those little dinette chairs aren't the most comfortable things in the world."

He was rewarded with a brilliant smile turned up at him full force, burning him like a bolt of lightening. With sinking clarity Tyler knew he was falling for this woman and he was going down fast and hard. The scars that covered him were no real protection for hazel eyes that seemed to look right through his skin.

"Oh Tyler, I'm so glad! I bought it from this woman, she looks pretty young and she has this little baby. I was trying to think how I was going to tell her I didn't want it after all, and I didn't think I had the heart to get my money back. It was obvious she needs the fifty dollars a lot more than I do," Emma rushed on, not knowing how her tender spirit was healing the scar tissue around Tyler's heart.

"Well, we best get going then." Tyler went into the cabin and returned with keys jingling. "Will there be somebody there to help load it up do you think?"

Emma's brows drew together in thought.

"I didn't see a man there, just the woman and the baby. Maybe the husband was inside. But I can help you. I'm sure the two of us together can lift it." She sent him a swift, questioning glance. "Oh, um, can you...?" she broke off, obviously uncomfortable with the question that popped into her mind.

"Yeah, I can lift, no problem," Tyler answered, surprised that her doubt didn't rile his temper. "But you aren't dressed for hefting furniture onto the bed of a dirty pickup." He raked her up and down with his eyes, liking all too well the vision of her and disliking the fact that he liked it so much.

"Oh this?" Emma held the sides of the skirt away from her thighs. "It's just a dress. If it gets dirty, I'll take it to the cleaners. No big deal. It's not even new. Matter-of-fact, maybe I'll try really hard to get a stain on it, then I'll have an excuse to go shopping." Her devious smile and lilting giggle plowed through the last of Tyler's defenses and he couldn't help but smile. His first real, full blown smile in a long, long time.

CHAPTER NINE

"So, no new vandalism in town I take it?" Tyler asked as they drove slowly to pick up the furniture.

Emma tensed. She didn't want anything to spoil the beautiful day. The fresh northern air blew in through the open truck windows, whipping Emma's hair around her face. She turned toward Tyler, hooking a wayward curl with a pinky and tucking it behind her ear. Was he playing dumb by asking? Emma hated herself for the thought and immediately crushed it.

"Did you hear someone slashed my tires?"

"You're kidding!" Tyler shot her a disbelieving look, wiping away the wispy veil of doubt that wanted to cling to her mind.

She quickly explained what had happened, not liking the stormy look that passed across his features but relieved by his concern. Tyler cared. To her way of thinking, that alone proved he was innocent.

Emma quickly reassured him that the town had been quiet for the past two nights.

"The sheriff had a stake out in the corner lot Friday night, but nothing happened. Then last night, Nate Sweeney, he's one of the local deputies, he asked me if they could put an officer in my house overnight. I agreed, but all was quiet on the Atlanta front again. I'm praying it's all over with." She didn't share with him the more disturbing detail, that he was considered a suspect by many of the locals, and Nate Sweeney himself. Hopefully he would never find out.

"How well do you know this Nate Sweeney?" Tyler asked, keeping his eyes steadily on the deserted dirt road. Emma laughed.

"Oh Nate, I've known him all my life. He's the local playboy. Well, I shouldn't say that," she amended. "He's a good Christian man, but he's played the whole field in these parts, always seems to be dating a new girl. Left a string of crying females from Alpena to Gaylord." Emma threw Tyler a smile and giggled.

"You should have heard my mom when I told her who was investigating the vandalism. The fact that it was Nate Sweeney gave her no comfort. She accused him of being more interested in looking in the mirror than solving crime. That's not really true. He's a good cop, just a little too handsome for his own good."

Emma couldn't help but think about what else her mother had said during that phone conversation. What would her mother say about this little outing today? Messed up in the head, the words came haunting one more time. Emma hated the image those words conjured up. She glanced over at Tyler. His head looked perfectly fine to her. His brow furrowed as he concentrated on driving and Emma's eyes fell on the ridge of scar visible beneath his golden hair. Yep, scar and all, Tyler McGillis looked way too fine to her.

There was no husband present at the slightly unkempt mobile home, so Tyler and Emma set to work loading the two pieces of furniture on their own. With a few grunts and a lot of giggles on Emma's part, they finally managed to wrestle the loveseat and chair onto the bed of Tyler's truck. The tired mother stood back and watched, the baby securely on her hip.

Emma waved out the window as Tyler pulled back out onto the road in a cloud of dust. Her dress was covered in a fine film of dirt, but she didn't care. The dress would be cleaned and she was having fun. How long had it been since she had just had plain and simple fun? Too long. She vowed to do it more often.

Both were quiet as Tyler made his way back to the cabin, lost in their own thoughts. Neither one were prepared for the small girl on the bicycle who darted out of an overgrown driveway on the right side of the road, bumping her way across right in front of Tyler's truck and back up into another drive-way on the other side. Tyler slammed on his brakes, the pickup skidding in the loose sand and gravel.

With a sharp intake of breath, Emma's hand clutched at her chest. The pickup came to a stop, bushes and trees brushing up again the passenger side.

"Oh my gosh, that was close! That silly little girl, she didn't even stop to look!" Emma exclaimed, still holding a hand to her racing heart. She glanced at Tyler.

He sat clutching the wheel in a death grip, his face as pale as milk, staring straight ahead as if not seeing the dash in front of him.

"Tyler?" Emma unhooked her seat belt and scooted across the bench seat. "Ty, you okay? Hey, it's alright, nothing happened." With a small hand she touched his chin, turning his face toward her. Wide, vacant eyes were framed by spiky gold lashes that were wet with—tears? Tyler's gaze looked through her and Emma knew he was seeing another accident.

"Come on Tyler, it's okay," she reassured again. "Put the truck in park, okay?" Tyler's foot still planted the brake pedal all the way to the floorboard and Emma reached across him to shove the gear shift into park. Tyler still had not blinked or spoken.

"Tyler, look at me!" She grasped his chin tighter and raised her voice. "That girl is okay. She rode off right up that driveway, you didn't hit her. Do you hear me, Tyler? It's okay!"

"I killed her," Tyler's voice was a whisper, seeming to come from a far away place inside him. He blinked once in slow motion, golden lashes falling to cover tortured green eyes.

"No, no." Emma shook her head. "You didn't

kill her Tyler, she's fine. She rode up that driveway."
She pointed over his shoulder, but knew he was in
another time and place. "Come on Ty, can you
change places with me?" Emma went to get out the
passenger door, noticing for the first time that the
truck was plastered up against the trees that grew
right up to the road. That wasn't going to work. She
turned back to Tyler.

"Scoot over toward me, Tyler. Let me get behind
the wheel and I'll drive us back to the cabin, okay?
Come on."

She tugged on his arm and slowly, as if in a
trance, Tyler began to move. Ungracefully, Emma
climbed over him, tangling her legs in the skirt of
her dress. Finally she was settled behind the wheel,
Tyler sitting like a statue beside her.

Perched on the edge of the seat to reach the
pedals, Emma put the truck in gear and drove
cautiously toward the cabin, praying fervently the
whole way.

Relief washed over Emma as she pulled into the
two track that led back to the cabin. Tyler had not
moved, had not spoken, had seemed to barely
breath, as she drove over the rough road and finally
parked in the small clearing next to her blue sedan.
Had it been a mere hour since she had first pulled in
here, excited over her garage sale find?

Putting the truck in park, Emma turned off the
engine and swiveled on the seat, facing Tyler. She
laid a gentle hand on his arm. His skin was clammy
despite the heat.

"Hey, Tyler, we're home." She bent forward to look at his face. Slowly his gaze turned toward her, realization of the present slowly dawning. He took a shaky breath. A trembling hand came up to cover his eyes. Without warning, he pitched forward, head resting on his knees as his body was racked with sobs.

"Oh Tyler." Emma scooted closer, wrapping her slender arms around his broad back, offering what little comfort she could as he wept. Laying a cheek against his shoulder, Emma prayed. Her heart twisted with Tyler's grief.

When his tears were spent, Tyler sat up, avoiding Emma's gaze by looking out the passenger window. He sniffed loudly and swiped a hand under his nose. Emma groped around on the seat for her purse. Finding it, she rummaged inside for her pocket size packet of tissues. She pressed them into Tyler's hand, waiting.

Grateful, Tyler extracted a tissue, his large tan hands making the little square of white cotton paper look ridiculously small. He wiped his nose then scooted down on the truck seat, his neck resting against the seat back, knee propped on the dashboard.

"I suppose you want to know what that was all about," he finally spoke, staring out the windshield at the trees behind the cabin. Black eyed Susans bobbed their heads in the slight breeze. A red tailed hawk swooped and glided in the blue sky, scanning the lake behind the trees for his meal. But Tyler saw none of it.

Emma didn't answer. She sat behind the wheel, leaning back against the driver's side door. So much pain. When, in her twenty-seven years had she ever seen so much pain?

"Do you know what I used to do for a living?" He spared her a quick glance then resumed staring straight ahead. "I was a paramedic. Trained to respond in an emergency and save lives. Three months ago, I took a life. A little girl who was nine years old."

Emma pictured the little girl on the bicycle. How old was she? Eight maybe, nine possibly. No wonder Tyler had reacted the way he had.

" We responded to a 911 call. I was driving," Tyler continued with his monologue, his voice colorless. "We always slow down, you know, at the intersections, and lay on the horn and siren, to make sure traffic is clear. I thought, I thought I had slowed down, but now, well, maybe I didn't. All I know is that a car jumped out in front of me and I broadsided her on the passenger side and when we spun, a truck hit me on the driver's side. I was thrown through the windshield, which is how I got all these scars." A finger came up and touched his cheek, then ran down his face, dropping to his arm the finger proceeded across his chest.

"The mother, she survived the accident, but her daughter." Tyler shook his head slowly, sadly, remembering. "Her name was Allison and she was nine years old. Because of me, she won't ever get to be ten." Hollow eyes once more turned to look at Emma, sitting with hands folded against her chest. "You tell me Emma, how does the God you love so much allow a nine year old to die while a scarred murderer lives on?"

"You aren't a murderer," Emma replied quietly, searching her mind for the right words to soothe his tortured soul. "I don't know why accidents happen, why some people die and some people live. But I do believe that God is always in control. What happened in that accident, God had a purpose for. It can be used for good somehow and someway."

Emma paused as she looked steadily at the handsome man sitting next to her. His face was red and wet with tears, his vulnerability only adding to his attraction. Emma's heart cried with him. What could she say that would free him from the guilt he felt?

"God wants to help you, Tyler. He wants you to turn to Him with this pain and sorrow. He doesn't want you to bottle it all up inside until you're paralyzed from it. Jesus said 'come to Me all who labor and are heavy laden, and I will give you rest.' He's waiting to take this burden from you and set you free to see the blessings that will some how come out of the ashes."

"But that's wrong! It's wrong for me to be blessed. It's wrong for me to heal. Why should I when a child is *dead*? What right do I have to go on living like she didn't matter?"

"She did matter. We have to believe that her death can be used for greater good. None of us know when our time will be. I could die in my sleep tonight. I have to believe my life counted for something while I was on this earth, and that hopefully my death will count for something, too. The Bible says that *all* things work together for good for those that love Jesus. All things. Good and bad. We don't know how this little girl's life and death affected others. Perhaps her dying made someone in the family think about eternity and turn to God. Perhaps one soul was saved because she died. We don't know. Only God knows and we have to trust that He knows what He's doing."

Emma scooted over on the seat and put a hand to Tyler's scarred cheek.

"You didn't murder that little girl, Tyler. You can't go on blaming yourself, you have to give it to God. And think, if all this hadn't happened, you wouldn't have come up here and we wouldn't have met. I already feel like we've become friends. I can't help but be glad that you came here. Maybe that's selfish, but it goes to prove that God can bring good out of even the worst situations. It's okay for you to go on living and be happy. Enjoy the gift of life and use it for good somehow."

Emma gave him a small, encouraging smile before sliding back over and opening the driver's side door.

Standing there, next to Tyler's truck, with meadow grass and white daisies reaching her knees, Emma felt so inadequate. All her life she had been so secure in her faith, sometimes to the point of condescension toward others. She thought she knew so much. But now, faced with Tyler's grief and pain and questions, Emma realized how little she really knew. Where were her pat answers and scripture quotes now?

Slowly Emma walked to the back of the truck

and lowered the tail gate. Tyler emerged from the cab and together they carried the loveseat and chair into the cool interior of the cabin, all the joking and light-heartedness of earlier gone. From her car, Emma retrieved the other items she had purchased and when Tyler reached for his wallet, she shook her head.

"No, you don't have to pay me back. Consider it a gift. Or, if you don't like that idea, maybe we can barter with something. Either way, I don't want money." Emma approached him, looking into his weary face. "Will you be okay? It's after lunch time, if you want, we could go into town and get a bite to eat."

Tyler shook his head.

"No, I'm okay. I'm not very hungry anyway. You go on. I'll be fine. And thanks, Em." Embarrassed, he looked away from her and cleared his throat. "Thanks for everything."

Emma waited for his eyes to meet hers before she finally responded with a small smile and a soft "you're welcome." With a heaviness in her heart she walked to her car and drove toward home.

CHAPTER TEN

Hot and covered with dust and sweat, Emma drove the familiar route into town, her mind barely registering where she was or what she was doing. It was only when she sat at the blinking light at the center of Atlanta that it hit her. It was a week until the Fourth of July and she had planned on spending this afternoon decorating the tea shop for the holiday.

The mere thought made her groan. She didn't feel like being patriotic and cheery. Right at this moment she wanted nothing more than a cool shower and about twelve hours of sleep. But the town was already bursting with patriotic fervor; the red, white and blue being proudly displayed in all business windows and hanging from each light post. She had to do her part, and if she didn't get to it today, she would never have the time.

At home she changed into jean shorts and a peach tank top, forgoing the shower until later. No point in getting too clean when she was just going to rummage in the garage for decorations and then stand out in the sun putting up the bunting outside the Spot of Tea. Twisting her hair into a quick ponytail, Emma jogged down the stairs and out the back door.

Long ago, the garage had been a carriage house. It still had a wide, swing back door at the front that Emma never used. She didn't bother to try and park her car in the cramped interior. Instead she used the building for storage, keeping extra tables and chairs for the shop that she found at sales. Along the back wall were metal shelves holding large plastic boxes full of decorations for all the holidays, and odds and ends of dishes and linens. As Emma inserted the key into the lock of the side door, it swung open unassisted.

Goose flesh formed on her arms and the delicate hairs on the back of her neck stood on end. She stood in the doorway, looking around the dim interior of the garage.

"Hello?" she called, feeling silly.

This was ridiculous! What would anyone want in her garage? Cautiously Emma walked across the threshold onto the cement floor that still smelled slightly of motor oil and glanced around furtively. There was no one in the garage, and there were no dark corners or crannies for someone to hide in. All the little tables and mismatched chairs seemed to be in place.

Emma thought back. When was the last time she had been in the garage? Last week when she had bought those old linens at a garage sale on her way back from Gaylord. She had come into the garage and put the table cloths in the box she kept just for that purpose. She simply must have forgotten to lock the door when she left. Satisfied with that conclusion, she went about finding the box packed with patriotic decorations and headed out to her car, this time making sure the door was locked securely behind her.

A loud rumbling from her stomach as she pulled into the parking lot of the Spot of Tea reminded Emma that she hadn't eaten anything since early that morning. The emotional scene with Tyler had chased all thoughts of hunger from her mind. Now all she wanted was a giant glass of mint iced tea and a chocolate chip muffin. Comfort foods.

Balancing the large box of flags and bunting in front of her, Emma walked to the back door and fumbled with her keys, trying to get the door unlocked. Unable to find the key hole without looking, she shifted the box to her left hip and looked down.

A bundle wrapped in green florist tissue lay on the stoop. Someone had sent her flowers! Emma smiled. Someone in town must be trying to cheer her up after all that had happened in the past week.

Emma set the box of decorations on the ground and reached for the bouquet, eagerly peeling back the tissue to peek inside. A breath caught painfully in her throat. The dozen roses, which had once been deep red where now brittle and black, the dried buds hanging limp and lifeless. A small card was tucked inside. Fingers trembling, Emma pulled it out, dropping the flowers as if they were a poisonous snake when she read:

These roses aren't red, these roses aren't blue, these roses are dead, soon you could be, too.

Leaving the flowers laying in the dust, Emma once more fumbled with her keys and the back door lock. Pushing the door open, she hurried to the kitchen phone, automatically punching 9-1-1.

In mere minutes Nate Sweeney pulled into the parking lot, Lydia Ebersol at his side. They entered the quiet tea shop to find a distraught Emma sitting at a table near the door.

"Hey Emmy, what is it?" Nate was immediately kneeling in front of her. Emma looked into familiar blue eyes, still not quite believing what she had seen.

"Someone left something on the back stoop I think you should see." She got up and led the two deputies out and around to the back of the building, pointing to the bundle of green tissue laying by the back door.

"What Emmy, you get flowers from an admirer you don't like?" Nate smiled over his shoulder.

"That's one way to put it." Emma stood back, as if the bouquet was a time bomb that could go off at any second. "They're dead flowers, Nate. And the card insinuates that I could end up the same way."

Nate squatted down and pulled a corner of the tissue back. Giving a low whistle he glanced around for the card which lay in the dirt where it had fallen.

"Who? Who is threatening me?" Emma shook her head in denial that this was happening. "I don't understand."

"I think we should call the sheriff. Lydia, go to the car will you and get Sheriff Traber on the phone. Come on Emma, let's go back in and sit down."

Lydia headed to the police cruiser while Nate took Emma's elbow and led her to the front door of the tea shop. Once inside the cool building, he gently guided her into a chair then took a seat across from her.

"Are you okay, Emma? Do you want me to get you anything, a cold drink or something?"

"No, I'm alright, I don't think I could put anything in my mouth right this minute." All thoughts of her earlier hunger had flown.

"Do you have *any* idea who might have done this, any at all?"

"No!" Emma shook her head vehemently. "I can't imagine who would do such a thing! I never..." She hesitated. "I never thought I had any enemies in this town. But now..." she let the thought trail off.

"We'll find out who it is, Emma. I've already given you my word."

"Well, at least this rules out Tyler," she said with relief.

"And why exactly is that?"

"Because I was with him all morning. After church, I bought some furniture at a yard sale for the cabin. I had to go get Tyler and then we went and picked the stuff up with his truck." She would never confide what else had happened out there on County Road 487.

"And then you came straight here to the shop?"

"No, I went home and changed. I was still

dressed for church. And I wanted to get the decorations." Startled eyes met Nate's. "The door to my garage, it was unlocked, it swung open when I touched it." A bolt of cold fear ran through her. Nate made a notation on his pad.

"But still, if you went home and changed, that would have given McGillis time to follow you into town and leave the flowers. Or he could have done it earlier. We don't know how long they've been there."

Emma cut him off before the doubts could creep back in to her heart. Tyler would never hurt her, he was hurting too much himself.

"Oh Nate, for goodness sake, would you please get real! Do you know what Tyler does for a living? He's a paramedic. A man trained to save lives. Not that much different from you. I really think he's a little too mature for spray painting and slashing tires. And leaving dead flowers, that has to be right off some t.v. detective show, the kind that teenagers watch."

Teenagers like Adam Pearson? Emma shoved the silent question aside. She didn't even know Adam Pearson. He couldn't possibly have any reason to threaten her.

Sheriff Traber was an imposing figure in his brown uniform and visored hat. But he treated Emma with difference, having known her since babyhood and having played more than one game of pinochle with her parents. He carefully went over all the events of the past week, from the shadow Emma thought she had seen going around the corner of her house up to her frightening discovery on the back stoop of her restaurant. Every detail was covered, then the flowers and card were taken as evidence.

"Is that all, Emma? Is that everything you can think of?" the sheriff asked one more time as he prepared to leave.

"Yes, I can't think of anything else." A picture of Adam Pearson flashed into her mind and Emma bit her lip. Should she mention Adam and the way he had watched her? Those two instances had taken on untold meaning, but Emma didn't want to give voice to them just yet. Not until she did some investigating of her own.

Emma accompanied the sheriff out of the shop, her heart sinking when she saw the small crowd that had gathered on the sidewalk pointing and whispering among themselves. Two cop cars in her parking lot on a quiet Sunday would be the talk of the town for awhile.

Nate and Lydia finished scouring the area and came back to stand beside Emma as the sheriff drove away.

"We've questioned just about everybody along the street, no one saw anything," Lydia said. "We should come home with you and check over your place real good too, just in case."

"And Emma, I think you should make some sort of arrangements for tonight," Nate added. "It's probably not a good idea for you to stay alone. We don't have the manpower to keep an officer with you at all times, although believe me, I wish we could."

"I know," Emma answered, slowly raising her

eyes to meet his.

She understood the double meaning in Nate's words. His feelings were written clearly in his glacier blue eyes and the worry lines that creased his forehead. It should have given her comfort. Instead, all it did was make her think of Tyler. How she wished she could run to him and hide behind his broad back. But Tyler had his own burdens right now, he didn't need to be saddled with hers, too.

So what was the answer? Emma couldn't think, had no idea who to call or what to do. Finally, in a voice that became stronger with determination she said, "I just have to count on the Lord to protect me, that's all there is to it."

CHAPTER ELEVEN

After Emma drove away from the cabin, Tyler stood listening to the stillness. The hollow rat-a-tat-tat of a woodpecker searching for his lunch in a dead tree broke the quiet. He sighed heavily, looking around. On the table were the things Emma had bought him; a tea kettle, a cast iron skillet and a picture for the wall.

He lifted the framed print and looked closer at the scene of a white tailed buck and doe standing in a clearing. The buck's head was up, his ears alert, as if looking for possible danger, ready to protect the doe at his side who grazed unconcerned. It was a simple picture, cheaply made, but it touched Tyler's heart. He felt a connection with the subject matter, with the buck looking to protect his mate. Tyler knew without a doubt that's what he wanted to do, protect Emma and keep her safe.

Spray painted graffiti. Slashed tires. What was next? Tyler didn't even want to think about it. He marveled at her calm. She didn't seem to be worried about it, he supposed he shouldn't be either.

Going to his tool belt, Tyler retrieved his hammer and went to the living room to hang the picture. He looked around at the furniture and the print in his hands as warmth washed over him. Emma had thought of him. She had seen these things and thought of *him*.

His mind flashed back to the scene in his truck. He could still feel Emma's arms around him. Why had they brought comfort when the touch from so many others had not? He had bitterly thrown off other arms that had reached to embrace him. There was a healing in Emma's presence, a peace she brought with her somehow. She would never know that today was the first time he had cried over the accident. Tyler felt cleansed, as if his tears had washed away much of the pain that had been weighing him down for so long.

The picture hung, Tyler stepped out on the front porch and resumed replacing the screen. Lost in a whirlwind of thoughts and memories, he forgot time until the heat of the day caught up to him. Changing into a pair of cut off jeans, he grabbed a towel and headed down to the lake for a swim. The cold water washed away the sweat from the day's work, just as his tears had washed away three months worth of muck that had built up on his soul.

Floating on the surface of the water, Tyler stared up at the deep blue sky and wondered. Wondered about the God Emma spoke of so easily and about the things she had said, that everything has a purpose.

Even a little girl's death? The thought seemed absurd. Tyler had grown up going to church, his parents still attended regularly, as did his two brothers. Did they believe the accident was all part of God's plan? Tyler couldn't remember them ever speaking about it that way, couldn't recall a single sermon from his childhood. Emma was different, she talked about God as if she knew Him. Her faith was more than a Sunday morning affair. It was real, personal. He had a sudden longing for the same thing.

Tyler still didn't understand it. Why would God take a nine year old child to further His plans on earth? But what if? What if Allison hadn't died in that accident? Where would Tyler be right now? He wouldn't be floating in the cold waters of a Michigan lake, that was for sure. He wouldn't have come to Atlanta and met Emma. And he certainly wouldn't be thinking about God. His childhood beliefs had fallen by the wayside a long time ago, replaced by more selfish ambitions and then destroyed entirely that fateful March day.

What had Emma said? That if Allison's death made one person turn to God, it wouldn't have been for nothing. Tyler smiled up at the shimmering blue sky, seeing it through different eyes. That's exactly what was happening! Maybe Emma was right, maybe it was time to turn to Jesus with all the questions and burdens that plagued him. Then maybe he really could heal and return home a whole man.

Refreshed, Tyler walked from the water and began toweling off. The distant sound of a car door slamming brought his head up, his heart lifting at the thought that Emma had returned. He stood still, expectation zigzagging through him as he waited to see her slender form emerge from the trail. He was quite disconcerted when a tall officer in a brown uniform parted the branches and walked out of the trees. Tyler immediately recognized him as the one from Emma's front porch.

"Are you Tyler McGillis?" the deputy asked as he approached.

"Yes, what can I do for you, Officer?" Tyler finished drying off then slung the towel around his neck.

"I'm Deputy Sweeney." Brilliant eyes raked Tyler up and down, measuring him. "I need to ask you a few questions, if you have a minute."

"Sure, what's this all about?" Tyler's heart raced. In slow motion he saw the girl on the bicycle that he had almost hit. Emma had assured him the girl was okay, that she hadn't even looked back after riding out into the road.

"Why don't we go on up to the cabin? It's a little more comfortable up there for official business." Nate turned and motioned for Tyler to proceed ahead of him up the trail.

Once back in the clearing, Tyler noticed another officer, a short, plump female, looking around the outside of the cabin, examining the work Tyler had done. He stopped in front of the deputy's car and turned to Sweeney.

"Am I under arrest or something?"

"No, no, nothing like that," Nate assured, holding himself aloof. "Why don't you go get dressed and we'll talk. I just have a few questions for you, concerning some things that have happened in town."

Alarm bells went off in Tyler's head. The girl on the bike was forgotten. His only thought now was Emma.

"Is Emma okay? Has something else happened?"

"Emma's fine." The female officer approached and set Tyler's mind at ease. She gave Nate a reproving look. "I'm Lydia Ebersol," she introduced herself. Tyler automatically reached out to shake her hand. "Why don't you go get dressed. We'll wait out here for you. We just have a few questions, it won't take long."

In moments Tyler was back in blue jeans and a navy T-shirt with the Toledo Fire and Rescue insignia on the front. He sensed the animosity emanating from the tall deputy.

"Want to tell me what this is all about now, Officer?" Tyler asked.

"First off, I'd like to know your whereabouts for this afternoon," Nate said.

"I've been here at the cabin all day. Well, except for a short time when Emma was here and we went to a garage sale to pick up some furniture." The image of the girl on the bike once more flashed through Tyler's mind. He shoved it back to the dark corner of his brain, unwilling to think about that close call right now. "I'm new to this area, so I can't even tell you what road we were on. If I could, the woman there would be able to vouch for what I'm saying. After Emma left, I've been here alone. I did some work inside then took a swim. Why?"

"Have you taken any trips outside of town? You know, to Mio, Gaylord, or Alpena?"

"Nope. I haven't ventured outside of Atlanta's corporate limits since I've been here. I've been a little busy." Tyler hooked a thumb over his shoulder toward the cabin.

"Hmm. If I asked for a copy of your receipts or bank records, any chance I'd find a purchase from a florist shop, for say, a dozen red roses?"

Tyler barked a short laugh. "I haven't exactly had time to go a courtin' since I've been here."

"Just answer my question, McGillis," Nate's voice was unrelenting.

"This is stupid." Tyler remembered what Emma had said, about Sweeney being a good cop. Tyler had to think he agreed with Emma's mother on this one. If Sweeney was in charge of the investigation into the vandalism, and these were the type of questions he was asking, the culprit would never be found.

"The only shopping I've done is at the hardware store and the grocery. Go ask them. Am I being investigated for plying someone with unwanted flowers?"

"Something like that."

"Look, this is ridiculous. I don't know anyone up here well enough to buy them flowers, but even if I did, where I come from that's not a criminal offense."

"What about knives? Say we were to execute a search warrant on the cabin, would we perhaps find a knife, about so long?" Nate asked, holding his forefingers about six inches apart.

Tyler felt rage building up inside him, the same hot, hard rage that had carried him through countless operations and months of physical therapy. He clenched his jaw and the scar on his face began to throb. He had come up here to try and reclaim his life, now he was going to have to defend himself to this back woods cop?

"You think I'm the one who slashed Emma's tires and spray painted the sidewalk? You've got to be crazy! But if you want to look around, go ahead. You won't find any cans of spray paint. I think there's a filet knife in the kitchen. It's about a hundred years old."

"That won't be necessary, but we appreciate the offer." Nate nodded. "Now, I'd like you to do me a favor." Nate pulled a piece of paper and a pen out of his breast pocket and laid it on the hood of the police car. "I need to get a sampling of your penmanship. Don't write in cursive though. Print. Block letters, please."

Tyler crossed his arms over his chest and stared coolly at the deputy.

"I don't think so, Deputy Sweeney. Not until I know what this is all about. I have rights. If I'm being charged with something, then you'd better spit it out and say so."

Nate took a step closer to Tyler, his blue eyes glittering like diamonds in the late afternoon sun. The brim of his hat nearly touched Tyler's scarred forehead.

"Look here, *Mr. McGillis,*" Nate ground out between clenched teeth. "I am the law here and I don't have to tell you anything. If you were under arrest, I would apprise you of your rights. Since that is not the case, I don't have to apprise you of anything. I am conducting a serious investigation into threats against Emma Dawson. If you don't wish to cooperate, then your status as a free man could change right quickly."

Tyler's blood turned to ice.

"Nate, back off." Lydia Ebersol stepped in, pushing her plump frame between the two men. "Come on, settle down. Now Mr. McGillis, would you please just give us a sample of your writing and we can get out of your hair."

"What are you talking about?" Tyler made no move toward the pen and paper. "Why were you asking me about flowers? Has something happened to Emma?"

"No, not yet." Lydia laid a calming hand on Tyler's arm. "But there was another threat against her. It happened today while she was away from the shop. She's fine. But we really do need a sample of your writing. It will make our investigation go that much faster."

"You think I'm threatening Emma?" Tyler's own eyes were hard as they bored into Nate's. "That's the most ridiculous thing I've ever heard. My aunt and uncle would have my hide if they thought I gave Emma so much as a headache. My aunt asked me to watch out for her, to keep her safe from this stupid vandal, and now I'm being accused of threatening her? You're wasting your time here officers. You should be out finding the person who is actually doing this."

The accusation cut like the knife that had slit Emma's tires. Tyler had almost gotten used to people looking at him as if he were something from a horror movie. He was coming to terms with the fact that he had killed someone. But he would never harm anyone purposely. How could these two stand here and think that he would? Did his disfigured face scream out "unhinged maniac?" Tyler remembered how Emma had laid her hand against his scarred cheek and looked deeply into his eyes, no pity or revulsion in her gaze. She knew his deepest, darkest secret and hadn't judged him How could anyone think he would do her harm?

"If you aren't the person threatening Emma, then you won't mind giving us a sample of your handwriting. We'll send it into the lab to be compared with the notes she's received and if they don't match, you're off the hook."

Nate once more motioned toward the pen and paper. Reluctantly, Tyler moved toward the cruiser, still trying to process the fact that Emma had been threatened again, and Nate thought he was to blame. Who was out to hurt her, and why was he a suspect? Leaning over, he picked up the pen and glanced up.

"Anything in particular you want me to write, Officer?" he asked, a note of bitter sarcasm slipping into his voice.

"How are you with rhyme? Remember, all caps. How about 'I'll give you a ride you won't ever forget'?"

The words gave Tyler a case of cold chills. He

did as he was asked, his mind on Emma. He handed the pen and paper back to the deputy.

"Thanks," Nate said, without appreciation. He moved toward the driver's door of the car while Lydia walked around to the passenger side.

"Wait a minute." Tyler stopped them. "What was with the questions about flowers? What does that have to do with anything?"

"Someone left a dozen red roses on the back step of the tea shop. Only problem was, they were dead. There was a note, too. These roses aren't red, these roses aren't blue, these roses are dead, soon you could be, too. Ring a bell?" Nate opened his door but made no move to lower himself into the seat. "Oh, and one more thing, McGillis. It isn't just your aunt and uncle who will have your hide if you hurt Emma. She so much as gets a scratch because of you, you'll have me to deal with. Remember that."

Two car doors slammed and the police cruiser backed up into the clearing then shot down the two track, leaving a billowing cloud of dust in its wake. Tyler stood rooted in the middle of the driveway. The full meaning of Sweeney's words settled over him like the dust that was drifting back to the grass. Dead flowers. A death threat. Petty vandalism had progressed to something much more sinister.

Why should he care? He hadn't known Emma Dawson long enough to get entangled in her problems. She had Nate Sweeney to protect her. It was obvious the deputy relished the thought of being Emma's knight in shinning armor and was more than willing to slay her dragons, especially if that dragon happened to be Tyler. Nate Sweeney was just what Emma really needed. The thought left him feeling like a stone had sunk to the pit of his stomach.

A bird sang out in the woods, the trilling notes echoing through the trees and reminding Tyler of Emma's infectious giggle, a sound he found himself liking far too much. He could see her hazel eyes looking up at him with so much trust. He did care, even if he knew he shouldn't.

Once more Tyler heard his aunt's entreaty that he keep Emma safe. She had the county's finest to do that, didn't she? Tyler's promise came back to nip at his conscience, but what good could he really do? Maybe it was time, he decided, to turn to the God Emma thought so highly of. Tyler realized that he and Nate Sweeney were going to need all the help they could get if someone was seriously out to hurt Emma.

* * *

A soft knock at the front door made Emma jump. Rhonda, who had agreed to stay with her overnight, looked across the kitchen table, her own face mirroring Emma's apprehension. The knock sounded again.

"People who want to do you harm don't normally knock on your door, announcing their arrival," Emma said, as much to reassure herself as Rhonda. She rose on unsteady legs and walked to the door, Rhonda close on her heels. She peered through the sheer curtain covering the front door window. Relief washed over her at the sight of Tyler standing on her porch.

"It's just Tyler." Emma couldn't keep a smile from her face as she unlocked the door.

"Maybe you shouldn't let him in," Rhonda said cautiously. "You know what Nate thinks, that he could be the one doing the..."

Emma spun around. Her fierce look cut off Rhonda's words.

"Rhonda, don't you dare even say it! I know exactly what Nate thinks and it isn't true. I don't want you spreading any of those awful rumors Jim Deland started."

"Okay, okay. Don't get so hot and bothered. I'm just here for your protection, remember? By all means, let him in. But don't say I didn't warn you." Rhonda turned and stalked back to the kitchen, her red hair bouncing with each indignant step. Emma finished unlocking the door, swinging it wide to let Tyler in.

"Hey, how are you doing?" she asked softly, looking up into his worried gaze. The memory of the emotional scene in his truck flooded back to her. With all that had happened since, she had forgotten about Tyler. Now, looking at him, every detail, every word from that painful hour burned in her mind and tugged at her heart. How could Rhonda, or anyone else, think this man would threaten her?

"I'm okay." He scratched the bridge of his nose. "I was a little worried about you though. I heard there was more excitement in town today while you were out at my place."

"And how did you find out about that?" Emma asked.

"Well, your Deputy Sweeney came out and paid me a visit this afternoon."

"He didn't! Oh that Nate, I *told* him!"

"It's okay, Emma. I was a little angry at first, but I realize he's got a job to do." The calm in Tyler's voice surprised Emma. Puzzled, she searched his eyes. He *was* calm. Something had changed since she had left him, what, seven hours ago? Had it only been that long? It seemed more like a week.

"Would you like to come in? Rhonda, she works with me at the shop, she's staying here tonight. Nate didn't think it was wise for me to be alone, considering." An involuntary shudder racked Emma's frame. Tyler reached out and rubbed a hand over her arm, a reassuring touch that spread a warm flush across her skin.

"Actually, I thought maybe we could talk. I've, uh, I've done a lot of thinking since this morning and I thought maybe, you know, we could just talk for a little while."

"Sure, I'd like that." Emma came out on the porch, closing the door behind her, and motioned to the settee. Tyler settled himself and Emma made herself comfortable on the opposite end, turning slightly to face him.

"So, what did Nate say to you when he came out?" Emma dreaded the answer. She didn't want Tyler to know about the suspicions some people had about him.

"He just wanted to know where I had been today. Then he asked me a bunch of questions, some of them about flowers, which made no sense to me, until he told me what happened." Tyler chuckled, the low sound sending a shaft of pleasure through Emma. He sat forward, resting his elbows on his knees and folded his hands.

"I was really worried about you. I kept thinking how scared you must have been when you found them. It's weird, you know, because it's been a long time since I've thought about what other people might be feeling, worried about what other people are going through. I've, well, I've been pretty consumed with my own problems for quite awhile. Anyway." Tyler slapped his thighs as if slapping down past memories and sat up straight. "He asked me to write something down for him, so they can compare my handwriting to the note you got."

"He didn't!" Emma nearly jumped up in fury. "Oh wait until I get my hands on Nate Sweeney! I told him and told him it wasn't you!"

Emma hit the back of the wicker furniture with a balled up fist. Her greatest fear had come to pass. As if Tyler didn't have enough guilt and pain to last a life time, now this, too.

"I'm so sorry, Tyler." Emma folded her legs and leaned toward him, wishing she could undo this whole day. "You shouldn't have to get involved in this. I know this isn't what you came up here for. You need rest and relaxation, not an investigation. I'm really sorry."

Emma drank in the sight of his profile. The scar on his cheek showed white against his tan skin. Breathlessly she waited for his wall of defense to come up, expecting him to draw into his cocoon of anger. Nothing happened. Instead, the eyes he turned to her still held that same measure of calm that she noticed upon first opening the door.

"You don't need to apologize. This isn't your fault. And maybe, well, maybe this *is* what I needed. For the first time in months, I'm not consumed with my own pain and problems."

Tyler relaxed back in the seat and stared off across the dark yard.

"I admit, Sweeney ticked me off at first. I mean, I'm human you know, no one wants to be accused of a crime he didn't commit." Green eyes turned to question her. "You know it's not me, don't you Emma?"

It was Emma's turn to lay a comforting hand on his arm.

"Of course I know that. I tried to convince Nate, but, like you said, he has his job to do. But there's never been a doubt in my mind."

Not that people hadn't tried to plant them there, Emma thought. Tyler nodded once and turned his attention back to the night beyond the porch.

"You said a lot earlier, you know, about God and how He works things for good, even if they don't seem good. I've been thinking about that and about the accident and everything that's happened."

Emma went still. Joy sprang up in her heart but she forced herself to wait, looking at his serious profile. When he swung his gaze to meet hers once more, she realized what was different. His eyes no longer held the haunted expression she had seen in them a week ago.

"After Sweeney left, I prayed. I haven't done that in a long, long time. When I was a kid, my parents always took us to church. They still go, but once I became an adult, I was too busy, too caught up in my own life. And then, after the accident, I was so angry. I hated myself. I guess I hated God, too, but mostly I just stopped believing. I didn't think He was really there, and if He was, then why? I went through surgeries, I went through re-hab. I didn't want to go on living, but I figured if I was going to live, then I would do it in my own strength. I thought that was all I had."

Tyler's hand came up to rub his forehead, his fingers lingering for a moment over the scar there. He shifted on the seat to face her fully.

"I thought these scars were my just punishment for what I had done. I was willing to live the rest of my life bearing the signs of my guilt, as if that would somehow pay the price for it. You've made me see that I don't have to carry it anymore. You know, even when I went to church, I didn't really know God the way you do. I want to know Him, I need to know Him. I was wondering if you would help me. I don't really know where to start."

"Oh Tyler, of course I will." Emma automatically reached over and took Tyler's hand in her own. Her heart danced a stutter-step as he wove his long fingers with hers. "This just proves how great the Lord is, because when I left you, I was convinced that I had completely messed up. I felt so inadequate, but the Lord was working. In our weakness, He is strong."

"I can't imagine you ever being weak." Tyler's eyes sparkled like the stars in the velvety night sky.

"Oh, trust me. I'm weak in plenty of areas. I get afraid and I fail like everyone else. I'm not perfect, just redeemed."

"Are you afraid now?" Tyler's thumb stroked over her knuckles sending tiny, shivering sparks up her arm.

"What do you mean?" Emma was finding it hard to breath or think.

"About the threat."

Cold reality brought Emma's spiraling emotions back to earth.

"Oh, that." She looked around her quiet yard, thought of the sleeping town just a block away. "A little. I don't understand why I'm the target. I keep asking who? Why? Sound familiar?" Her eyes locked with his and she smiled.

"But I do trust the Lord. You can too. You know, you talk about these scars you carry." Emma leaned forward and traced the white line down his cheek. "Jesus carries scars, too. The price He paid for our sin. Whenever you look in the mirror, instead of thinking of what you've done, think of Jesus and what He's done. Now come on." Reluctantly Emma got up and pulled him with her. "I'll give you a Bible to take home with you. The best thing you can do is read, read, read. Then next Sunday, maybe we could go to church together."

She stopped at the door and turned to look up at him, unable to read the expression on his face. Realizing her hand was still entwined with his, she pulled it free. The warmth that had enveloped her seemed to drip from her fingertips.

"I think I'd like that Em, very much."

She couldn't speak through the tangled knot of emotion that blocked her throat. She merely nodded and opened the door. After Emma found him a Bible, they stood once more on the front porch, Tyler reluctant to leave.

"I wish I could stay and keep an eye on things," he finally admitted. "I don't like you being here alone."

"I'm not alone remember, I have Rhonda here. And the Lord is always with us. We'll be fine. This will be the first small test of your newfound faith. Now go on." Emma watched as his long legs carried him down the porch steps. Halfway down the walk, he turned.

"I'll come in to town tomorrow to check on you."

Emma's heart lifted and took wing at the simple promise. Smiling, she returned his small wave, watching as he climbed into his pickup parked at the curb. Tomorrow. A whole new day.

CHAPTER TWELVE

Rhonda was at Emma's side when she unlocked the door of the Spot of Tea at five a.m. the next morning, grumbling good-naturedly about rising before the morning dove gave its first gentle coo. But she was serious about her bodyguard duties and wouldn't lay in bed and let Emma venture to the shop alone.

The night had been quiet and, to Emma, the day before seemed like a dream. Had she dreamed up Tyler, too? Was it her imagination that had conjured up the warmth of his hand holding hers? The thought of Tyler brought a smile to Emma's face, erasing the lines of tension that furrowed her brow. The thought of someone lurking out there, waiting for a chance to hurt her, sent tendrils of fear curling up her spine.

The two began preparing for the morning business. As Emma started her normal routine of baking she gladly handed over the box of Fourth of July decorations to Rhonda, instructing her to put them up any way she saw fit.

The gay red, white and blue bunting served as a reminder of the day before and Emma grew pensive once more. She jumped nervously at every sound outside the shop. The loud roar of the trash truck pulling into the parking lot to empty the dumpster set Emma's heart to pounding. Her legs shook so hard she had to grope for a tall kitchen stool and sit down before her weak knees collapsed.

This was madness! Emma took several deep, steadying breaths. Oh, it had been so easy last night, to reassure Tyler. But here, alone in her kitchen in the light of a new day, anxiety resurfaced. Who had she ever hurt or offended? A wave of panic rose up within her breast. What if Nate didn't catch whoever was doing this?

An image of Adam Pearson flitted across her mind. Was he responsible? With sudden clarity a scene replayed in Emma's memory. She had been walking down the sidewalk when Adam had come toward her, walking with that slouching gate of his. Before they could cross paths she had crossed the street to go into the variety store. Something made her look over her shoulder. Adam stood in the middle of the sidewalk, glaring after her. No wonder the day he was sitting behind the tea shop his look was so familiar. The same anger and resentment had screamed from every pore of his body.

Had Emma slighted him in some way? She couldn't recall ever having spoken more than a dozen words to the boy in the course of his lifetime.

The thought that he could be her enemy was unsettling. Confusion, worry and paranoia fought a three way battle for control of her thoughts.

She had to pray. Sitting atop the stool, Emma bowed her head and cried out to the Lord. She repeated the words from the book of Joshua. *Be strong and of good courage; do not be afraid, nor be dismayed, for the Lord your God is with you wherever you go.*

Hadn't she told Tyler that very same thing last night?

A light shone in the darkest recesses of her heart, driving out the anxiety that wanted to settle there. With renewed strength she hopped down from the stool and went back to work, preparing for her morning customers. Business would proceed as usual, no matter what was happening out there in the big, bad world.

News of Sunday's excitement had not yet reached the general population of Atlanta, but the Sheriff's visit alone was enough to keep gossiping tongues wagging throughout the day. As Emma fielded customer's questions, determination straightened her spine. She would not be a victim, and the more she reassured her customers, the more sure she herself became.

The loving concern of her regulars seeped into Emma's soul. This was why she loved her hometown. It was so good to belong, to share roots and history. Suddenly it didn't matter so much that somewhere was one person trying to scare her. Inside her shop were dozens of people, many she had known all her life, who were all watching out for her.

When Kirt and Jesse knocked on the kitchen door after lunch, Emma let them in with a smile, praising the bucket of blueberries they presented to her with pride. Their arrival served as a reminder of the week before and Adam Pearson's presence behind the shop.

"Hey guys, I need to ask you a question." Emma handed each boy his hard earned pay and looked at them earnestly. "What do you know about Adam Pearson?"

The boys exchanged a quick glance before looking down at their scuffed tennis shoes. Each was suddenly engrossed in folding and refolding the bills in their hands. Emma sensed their discomfort, and was that guilt in their expressions?

"Look guys, I need to confide something to you." Emma opened the kitchen door and motioned for the boys to go out. She led the way to the tables behind the shop. When she turned she saw she had their full attention. She knew both boys thought highly of her, maybe even had a little bit of a crush. Emma wasn't beyond using that knowledge to her advantage.

"I'm going to tell you boys something that isn't common knowledge around town yet, and I need you to promise me you'll keep it between us." Emma perched on the table, smoothing the skirt of her yellow sundress over her knees. Both boys nodded solemnly.

"We swear, Miss Dawson," Kirt said seriously.

"Yesterday someone left a bouquet of roses over

there on the kitchen stoop." Emma pointed toward the door. "But these weren't pretty, sweet smelling flowers like from a boyfriend. They were dead. And there was a card saying soon I could be dead, too."

Disbelief registered on each young face.

"Who would do something like that?" Jesse asked.

"You think Adam had something to do with it?" Kirt, who at fifteen, was older than Jesse by nearly a year, caught on quickly.

"I don't know Kirt, I hope not. But remember last week, when you guys brought the last batch of blueberries?" Both boys nodded. "Adam was sitting out here at the picnic table, staring at the shop. And then, well, I've seen him watching me a few different times. I just got to wondering about him, that's all. Do you boys know much about him? Last week you said he was weird. What exactly does that mean?"

Again the boys exchanged a guilty look.

"He's just different." Kirt shrugged a slim shoulder and scratched at his tank top covered chest. "He should of graduated this year but he didn't 'cuz he keeps failing. He skips school all the time, but when he does go, he stays by himself. If you talk to him, he just sort of growls at you, like some sort of animal. He never tries out for the football team or goes to any of the school stuff. He dresses like a hobo, and he *stinks*!"

"Yeah, it's gross!" Jesse wrinkled his nose.

"So he gets picked on a lot?" Emma read the answer in the sheepish look that passed between the two. She decided to forgo the lecture on 'loving your neighbor as yourself' for now. "Anything else you can tell me?"

"His mom works at the grocery store," Kirt imparted a fact that Emma already knew. "They live on Airport Road, but I don't think his mom is home much."

"He's got this little hideout, out by Lake Fifteen, by the old campground. It's so pathetic, but he thinks he's really somethin' having a hideout," Jesse said in disgust. Kirt looked at him in surprise.

"How do you know about a hideout, worm face? I never heard about no hideout," Kirt questioned with suspicion. "You never told me nothin' about any hideout."

"I saw him out there one time, when my dad took me fishing." Jesse swelled with importance at having Kirt and Emma's full attention. "He was coming down off the ridge when we pulled in. After we came back from fishing, while my dad was loading up the boat, I told him I needed to, you know, so I went up the ridge and I poked around in the bushes until I found this little hideout. It might have been a deer blind or something at one time. I said something to him at school about it and he just about punched my lights out. Told me I better keep my trap shut. If anyone came poking around his stuff, he'd know who had told and I'd be a dead duck."

"Still, you could have told *me*," indignation laced Kirt's words. "We could have had all kinds of fun!"

"Kirt, that is not funny," Emma reprimanded gently and the teen hung his head. "Look, I need to get back to work, but I appreciate all you've told me. Remember what I said though, this is all just between us, okay? I won't mention the hideout." She looked at Jesse and he visibly relaxed. "And you won't mention what I told you about the roses. Or mention to anyone that we had this little discussion, deal?"

The boys nodded their agreement and Emma climbed down from the top of the picnic table, wiping off the back of her skirt as she headed for the kitchen door. "Thanks for all your help boys, and the blueberries. If you hear anything else that would help me out, let me know."

Business was light after Emma's talk with the boys. She found she could no longer make small talk with the smattering of customers. Her mind was preoccupied with her growing suspicion of Adam and the things Kirt and Jesse had told her. By three o'clock she could no longer stand the inaction. Knowing Rhonda was capable of handling the few customers that remained, Emma told her she had an errand to run and quickly made her way out the kitchen door and to her car.

Would Doreen even be home this time of day? Emma wondered. Maybe Adam would be there. A cold shiver skimmed across Emma's skin. What would she say if the disgruntled teenager answered the door? She had no idea, but she had to do something before she went crazy with waiting. If she could just get some sort of evidence to take to Nate, then the town could rest easy again and Tyler would be cleared from all suspicions. Determination straightened Emma's shoulders as she turned the key in the ignition.

Airport Road ran parallel to Atlanta's main street, a mere block to the south. If it wasn't for the Thunder Bay river being sandwiched between the two, Emma could have walked the short distance from her shop to the back door of the Pearson home. As she pulled into the drive of the dilapidated clapboard house, Emma immediately realized that Adam could easily make the trek through the trees and across the river to the Spot of Tea. There were many areas where the river ran shallow, and a teenage boy could easily wade across. The close proximity of his house and her shop meant that Adam could be spying on her every day. Gooseflesh formed on her arms despite the heat.

Emma's eyes traveled around the unkempt yard. The sagging front porch was surrounded by small mountains of trash, discarded appliances and tattered lawn furniture. Her heart wept at the pitiful sight. Even the bright summer sun could not dispel the sadness and gloom that hung like a pall over the rundown home and its yard full of junk. What a joyless place for a boy to grow up.

Taking a deep breath, Emma forced herself to push open the car door. She made her way carefully to the rickety porch, trepidation mounting as she climbed the creaky stairs and walked gingerly to the front door. Regretting now the impulse that had driven her here, Emma knocked timidly, jumping back when the front door slowly swung open. She put a hand to her thundering heart as if she could steady its pace.

A face barely emerged in the crack between the front door and the screen.

"What do you want?" a voice spoke from behind the door. "You selling Avon or something? I don't buy nothin' door to door."

"No, I'm not selling anything. It's Emma Dawson, I own the tea shop in town. Actually Mrs. Pearson, I was wondering if I could talk to you for a minute." Emma's heart settled into its normal rhythm as she peered through the dirty screen, trying to get a better look at the furtive figure hiding behind the door. Several seconds passed before the door swung wider and a frail hand extended to open the latch on the screen door.

"I guess you can come in for a minute, although I'm not fit for having visitors." Doreen turned her back as Emma stepped into the dim interior of a cluttered living room.

"I wasn't sure you would even be home." Emma hid her trembling hands in the skirt of her dress. "I know you work most days at the grocery, so I really didn't expect to find you here. I just took a chance."

"Yeah well, I called in sick today." Doreen was slow to turn around. She toyed with a tendril of lanky brown hair hanging beside her face. When she finally turned, Emma's sharply drawn breath echoed in the cramped room.

"Doreen, what in the world happened to you?" Emma rushed toward the gaunt figure, eyeing the black and purple bruises on the left side of Doreen's face that her hair could not hide.

"It's nothing, really." Doreen waved a hand in dismissal. "I just had a little accident at the store yesterday, that's all. I was up on a ladder, stocking some of the higher shelves, and I lost my balance and fell. Some canned goods came down with me. It looks worse than it is."

When Doreen refused to meet Emma's gaze she knew the older woman was lying. But what else could have happened? Doreen's husband had left for parts unknown ten years ago, and as far as Emma knew, the woman had never taken up with anyone else. She worked hard trying to support herself and Adam, not taking government handouts or charity from the community. It was easy to forget, looking at her care worn features and thin frame, that Doreen was not an old woman, only in her mid to late thirties. She carried the hardships of her life on her stooped shoulders and lined face.

"Anyway, Miss Dawson, what can I do for you? Since you and I have never spoken outside the grocery store, I have to think this is more than just a social call." Doreen once more turned away from Emma. Making her way to a wooden rocking chair, she gingerly sat down.

Seeing the woman's battered face, Emma didn't know if she had the heart to bring up the subject of Adam. But the seed of suspicion in her mind sprouted and blossomed. Perching on the edge of a worn sofa Emma prayed for guidance.

"Have you seen a doctor? Those bruises look pretty severe, and if heavy cans hit you in the face, you could have some serious injuries." Her concern was genuine, even if she didn't believe the woman's story as to how she was hurt. Once more Doreen dismissed Emma's worry with a wave of her hand.

"I don't need to see no doctor. Couldn't afford one, even if I did." As she looked Emma up and down, judgement settled in her faded brown eyes. "Seems I've lived a long time without your worry, sure don't need it now."

The sharp sting of the words cut Emma to the quick. It was all too true. When was the last time she had given Doreen Pearson the time of day? She saw the woman infrequently when she stopped in at the local supermarket. Emma did most of her shopping at the bigger stores in Gaylord so her contact with the Pearson family was seldom and brief. They did not attend the same church or belong to the same social circle of friends. As her mother had said, they weren't the kind of people Emma's family normally associated with.

Conviction settled on her heart as she looked at the battered woman across the room. She had known of Doreen's struggles. It was common knowledge in town, everyone talked about it. Everyone, even her mother, knew that Adam was a handful, yet who had reached out to this family? Emma felt suddenly ashamed.

"I suppose you're right," Emma agreed, not knowing how to right her past wrongs. That would have to wait for another day. "You've done okay for yourself without any help from me. And I didn't come here to offer you pity. Actually, I was wondering if Adam was home."

Emma's keen gaze did not miss the apprehension that stole over Doreen's plain face or the wary look of fear that crossed her features before she turned her gaze out the front window.

"Adam don't hang around home much in the summer," she offered lamely. "He's eighteen now you know, and would rather be out and about exploring the world." When Doreen turned her face back toward Emma, the weary brown eyes were shuttered, revealing nothing. "Is he in some sort of trouble?" she finally managed to ask.

"I don't know Doreen. I thought maybe you could tell me. I'm sure you know there's been a few things going on in town," Emma gently reminded. "I've seen Adam hanging around here and there and I was worried about him, that's all."

"Lots of kids hanging around in town. I see it every day at the grocery store."

"That's true." Emma nodded, not adding that most of them did not hang around outside the Spot of Tea. It was interesting though, that Doreen must have known she was referring to the vandalism and yet she didn't immediately jump to her son's defense. Emma realized she had to tread cautiously or what she came here to accomplish would backfire entirely.

"I just got a little worried about Adam because he always seems to be alone," Emma picked her words carefully. "And lately he's seemed a little angry at the world. I just thought maybe you should know about it."

"Adam's just going through some growing pains

right now," Doreen said softly, her eyes focused on some point beyond the front window. "He's just at a hard age. He'll come around and be fine. He just needs the summer to sort himself out."

Emma wanted to ask if this "hard age" included him hitting his mother up side the head, but found she didn't have the courage to speak the words aloud. She glanced at her watch. It was closing time at the shop and she had to get back and finish up her daily chores.

"Well, I just wanted you to know that I was worried about him. You'll let me know if you need anything, won't you?" Emma asked, knowing Doreen would do no such thing. The woman gave a vague nod of her head and Emma rose from her seat. "It's been good talking to you. I hope you'll reconsider and have a doctor look at those bruises."

Doreen rose from her ancient rocker and followed Emma to the door. Emma looked over her shoulder as she stepped out onto the porch, trying to convey her concern with a meaningful glance. Finally she reached out and gave Doreen's shoulder a brief squeeze.

"I meant what I said, Doreen. I know we haven't been the closest of friend in the past, and I'm sorry for that. Just know you can call me if you need *anything*." With that she made her way back to her car, suspicion and worry growing with every step.

Tyler turned his dusty black pickup into the parking lot of the Spot of Tea and turned off the engine. Anticipation bubbled up within him at the thought of seeing Emma but his heart quickly sank when he didn't see her car in the lot. He had waited until closing time, wanting to spend time alone with her. Was he too late or had she walked to work again?

A county patrol car pulled in and parked next to his truck as Tyler climbed from the cab. Dislike sizzled in the hot air as Nate Sweeney exited the cruiser. The two men eyed each other with open hostility as they made their way to the door.

"After you, McGillis." Nate motioned for Tyler to proceed ahead of him into the cool interior of the restaurant, his blue eyes glittering with antagonism beneath the brim of his hat.

"Well, thank you Deputy, that's mighty kind of you." Tyler gave a mock salute, his deep green gaze mirroring the animosity in Nate's own. The plate glass door swung shut behind them and both men looked around the dining room, waiting for Emma to appear.

"Hey Rhonda, Emmy around?" Nate swung his piercing gaze toward the redhead who had come from the kitchen at the sound of the bell. Tyler watched as the deputy flashed a pearly white smile that the girl quickly returned.

"She left over an hour ago," Rhonda answered before moving back toward the kitchen. "She said she had an errand to run. I expected her back by now." She glanced up at the clock as she plunged her hands into the huge stainless steel sink filled with soapy dish water.

"Where did she go?" Nate's voice remained even but his face showed instant concern. For the first time, Tyler felt in tune with the deputy as his own worry for Emma's safety rose up within him.

Rhonda looked at them over her shoulder as she continued to wash the delicate china cups and saucers.

"She didn't say," she answered, realization slowly dawning in her blue eyes. Uneasiness seemed to creep over her as she pulled her hands out of the dish water and dried them on her apron. "But she's only been gone an hour. That's not so unusual. You don't really think there's anything to worry about, do you?"

"Considering what happened here yesterday, I would say that her running around town unescorted is not the best idea in the world," Nate said, censure in his tone. "She should at least tell you where she's going and when she'll be back. Anything unusual happen today?"

Rhonda shook her head, making her curly pony-tail swing.

"No, not a thing. Business as usual. It was pretty quiet this afternoon, which is why Emma said she was going to go out for awhile."

"Are you staying with her again tonight?" Tyler asked.

"Yes, but this should be the last night. She called her parents and told them about the threat. She asked them to come up and stay with her for awhile. They were already planning to come up soon anyway, this just gave them a reason to set a firm date. They should be here by tomorrow afternoon. I think we'll all breath a lot easier once Carolynn is in town guarding the nest." Rhonda laughed and turned back to her dishes.

"Well, that's good, great." Nate nodded his approval. "It will help me sleep sounder at night knowing she's got her dad there in the house with her. Tell Emma I stopped in to check on things. Have her call me, will you?" Rhonda nodded her affirmative without turning from the sink. "Tell her I said that from now on she's to tell someone where she's going and when she'll be back. Better yet, tell her I said she isn't to be going anywhere alone."

"Tell her yourself, Sweeney," Rhonda called as Tyler followed Nate back through the front of the shop.

Out in the parking lot, Tyler sat in the cab of his truck while the deputy pulled his cruiser back out onto Main Street. Tyler didn't miss the belligerent scowl Nate threw his way before heading into town. Nate Sweeney's dislike of him was not foremost in Tyler's mind. Instead all he could hear was Rhonda's voice informing them that Emma's parents were on their way. Once they were here Emma would have plenty of protection, and his promise to Aunt Mabel would be null and void. Tyler would no longer have an excuse to hang around Emma.

It was just as well, Tyler told himself. He was only here for the summer. He was supposed to concentrate on getting better, physically and mentally, so that he could return to work by fall. But what about the feelings Emma was stirring inside him? A flame burst to life in his heart each time he thought of her.

Tyler knew with the slightest push he could fall in love with Emma Dawson, was already half-way there. But to what end? She had a thriving business here, a beautiful home that she had worked hard for. She had roots here and he had a job in the city that he was determined to return to. Proving that he could still do that job had been the driving force behind his every move for the last two months. He couldn't let anything divert him from that goal.

Downhearted, Tyler turned the key in the ignition and backed out of the parking space. Turning left onto Main Street he headed back toward the cabin, knowing that now that Emma's parents were coming to town, he had to keep his distance from her. He still had plenty of work to do on Uncle Milt's cabin and it was time he got his mind back on why he had really come to Atlanta.

the receipts in front of her. "Tyler is merely a family friend, that's all. And Nate Sweeney and I have known each other forever. If either one of them feels protective, that's why."

"Sure, sure, keep telling yourself that if you want to. Personally, if it was me, I'd be enjoying every minute of it." Rhonda got up from her chair and headed back toward the kitchen. "Doesn't the Bible say something about lying though, even if it is only to yourself?"

* * *

Tyler sat in the shade in his newly purchased lawn chair, untangling fishing line when Emma's car pulled into the yard. His heart skipped several beats at the site of her climbing from the car dressed in denim shorts and green tank top. Stop it, he told himself, trying to brake his runaway emotions. Stop reacting to this woman! His stubborn heart refused to listen as she walked through the tall grass toward him.

"Hey, I'm sorry I missed you earlier."

Tyler slanted a quick look up at her before resuming work on the knot of fishing line in his lap.

"You shouldn't be going anywhere alone. Didn't Nate make that clear?" His voice echoed gruffly in his own ears.

Emma crossed her legs and folded herself down onto the grass at his feet. The look she gave him made his hands still. Her parents are coming tomorrow, Tyler reminded himself. She doesn't need you any more. She'll have them and Nate Sweeney to watch over her.

"Are you angry at me?" The soft question cut like a knife into his heart.

"Yes! No!" Tyler shoved the fishing pole away and jumped from his chair. "I don't know what I'm feeling anymore!" He turned away from her, hands on hips.

"Good, because that makes two of us."

Tyler glanced over his shoulder at the woman sitting so comfortably in the grass, a small smile playing about her lips. His heart cartwheeled again. He wanted to be angry with her but found he could no longer keep his defensive wall up. With a resigned sigh he came back to his chair and picked up his fishing pole once more just to keep his hands off her. He ignored the possible implication in her words and changed the subject.

"So, where were you earlier? Rhonda didn't know where you had gone."

"I just had something I needed to check on." She dropped her gaze to her lap.

"Hmmm. I don't like the sound of that. This thing you went to check on, does Nate know about it?" The knot undone, Tyler lifted the fishing rod and began reeling in the line. He looked down at the top of Emma's bent head, knowing she was hiding something from him.

"No. It didn't have anything to do with Nate. Why is everyone giving me the third degree about it?" Emma lifted her head and met his gaze once more, a stubborn tilt to her chin.

"Maybe because they care about you. Ever think

of that?" The truth rang clear in his words and Emma's shoulders fell.

"I know," she admitted. "It's just, all this having to tell people where I'm going and have an escort all the time. I hate it. I felt like a criminal trying to shake a police tail getting rid of Rhonda so I could come out here to see you." The breeze playing through the leaves seemed to carry her sigh as she yanked tufts of grass from the ground. "And now you're mad at me, too."

"I'm not mad at you," Tyler reassured her, sorting through the hurricane of emotions that spun within him.

Part of him wanted to admit his growing feelings for her, bring it all out in the open where they could deal with it. He decided against it, reminding himself that he was leaving at the end of the summer. Nothing could come of a summer fling. Emma was a forever kind of woman. He rose from his chair and gathered up the fishing pole.

"I was just getting ready to go out fishing. Want to come?"

The invitation startled Emma into looking up at him.

"You're sure you aren't mad at me?"

Tyler reached down a hand and pulled her to her feet, resisting the impulse to pull her straight into his arms. "I'm sure," he managed to say between heavy beats of his heart.

Milt's old aluminum canoe had been left chained to a tree behind the cabin. Earlier in the day Tyler had wrestled it from its nest of weeds and overgrown grass down to the lakeshore. As they floated on the calm surface of the lake, Emma sat on the forward seat, watching him cast his line.

"I'm sorry I upset you earlier," Emma apologized.

"You didn't upset me." Tyler kept his eyes on the bobber that floated several yards from the canoe. "But Nate is right you know, you shouldn't be going anywhere by yourself. Not even out here to see me. It could be dangerous."

"I think the danger is way overblown. And I feel safe with you. I know you wouldn't ever hurt me. I trust you."

Her words were like bitter medicine, healing yet hard to swallow. It was wonderful to have her trust, even if it was undeserved. Tyler knew his feelings toward her had the potential of hurting them both.

"Be careful, Em. I think we're both treading awfully close to the fire here. I'm a real man, not some cardboard storybook hero. I'm afraid one of us in going to get burned." He saw her eyes widen in surprise before she looked away from him, out across the lake. "Rhonda said your parents are arriving tomorrow. I think that's best for everyone."

"I'm not sure I understand what you're saying." The way she refused to meet his eyes told Tyler she knew more than she wanted to admit.

Tyler tried to straighten out his tangled thoughts like he had the fishing line. He decided to make his position clear.

"Your parents will be able to keep an eye on you. You won't need me to help you feel safe anymore."

He looked down the length of the canoe, pinning her with his brilliant gaze. She was so innocent, so vulnerable. Love welled up within him as Tyler ruthlessly wrestled it down. "Emma, I'm not staying forever. I'm going back to my job at the end of the summer."

"I, I know that," Emma stumbled over the words. She looked down at the hands she was twisting in her lap. "I'm sorry. I wasn't trying to lead you on. I didn't mean to…" her words trailed off as she bit her lip. Moments passed before familiar determination straightened her shoulders and she looked boldly back up at Tyler. "I never needed you to keep an eye on me." She raised her chin a notch. "I have the Lord for that, remember. And half of the whole blasted town. I enjoy your company. I'm sorry if I've made you uncomfortable. I thought we were friends. If I was wrong then just paddle back to shore and I'll get out of your hair." Emma picked up her paddle as if to start rowing toward shore.

"No! Emma, really." He reached out a hand to stop her.

Tyler knew he had messed up, was close to ruining everything. He searched his mind for a way to make it right. She wanted to be friends but could he keep his runaway emotions in check for the entire summer? It probably would be best for both of them if he did as she asked, paddled back to shore and let her walk out of his life forever. He couldn't make himself do it.

"I'm sorry, Em. I do consider you a friend and I enjoy your company. Too much. I thought you should know where I stand. I don't want you to end up hurt."

"Nobody seems to realize it, but I am a big girl, Tyler. I can take care of myself. I've known all along that you're only here for the summer." Emma put the paddle down and relaxed back against the bow of the canoe. "Tell me about your job."

Tyler slowly reeled in the fishing line and recast, his mind spinning back into the past as the bobber spun through the air. It settled onto the water with a loud plop.

"I love my job. It's the only thing I've ever wanted to do. But since the accident, I've been consumed by fear." It was a relief to admit it aloud. "All I want is to go back to work, but the truth is, I'm afraid I'll never be able to do it again. The thought of getting back into the cab of a rescue truck, I don't know if I have it in me anymore."

"Oh, Tyler."

"I want to go back to work," he said adamantly. "More than anything, I want to prove to myself that I can still do it. That the accident didn't strip me of everything."

"Then that's what we'll pray for. If it's the Lord's will, He'll make a way."

He's leaving, Emma repeated to herself over and over as she lay in bed that night. The normally comforting chorus of crickets singing in the garden below her window brought no solace to her heart. She had known all along he wasn't staying forever, so why did it hurt so much for him to remind her?

It was for her own good. Emma cringed at the thought. As if she wasn't a grown woman, able to look out for herself. She had no one but herself to blame. What must Tyler think of her? She had constantly been foisting herself on him since he arrived, involving him in her problems. Allowing her heart to get tangled with feelings for him, a stranger who wasn't even staying around.

The twisting, twirling thoughts jumbled in her mind. Tomorrow her parents would arrive and hopefully, once they were here, her world would stop spinning. Soon it would be the Fourth of July and town would be overflowing with people. The shop would be doing a booming business, which would give her plenty to think about besides the threat, besides Tyler.

They had parted on friendly terms. Isn't that what Emma wanted, to be friends? Her mind said yes, her heart said no.

Maybe it was just physical attraction. Tyler was extremely good looking, despite the scars. And those eyes! Whew, enough to send any woman's heart a flutter. But if it was just physical attraction, then she would have felt that way about Nate, who no one could deny was the handsomest thing in Montmorency County, at least until Tyler showed up.

Emma flung herself onto her side, exhausted from all the emotional exercise. It didn't really matter what kind of attraction it was, the fact still remained he was leaving at the end of the summer. Tyler had warned her they were playing with fire, which told her he was having the same battle with himself. The best thing to do was just stay away. That's what a friend would do.

CHAPTER FOURTEEN

Dawn ushered in a perfect northern Michigan day. The sky was a clear sapphire blue. The sun shone down with gentle warmth, encouraging Atlanta residents to step outside and breath in the fragrant air. Locals and visitors alike took advantage of the beautiful weather to go into town to visit the park, the produce market or the shops. The Spot of Tea was standing room only. Even the picnic tables out back were full.

The familiar tinkling of the bell over the door rang out for the hundredth time that day. Emma continued to take a customer's order until she heard an excited cry of greeting.

"Well, look who's here!" someone said in surprise. "Ed, we haven't seen you in a coon's age!"

A radiant smile broke across Emma's features as she quickly turned away from the customers at the corner table, toward the front of the shop. There in the doorway stood her mother and father.

"Daddy!" Emma rushed into her father's embrace. After a tight hug, she was passed to her mother's comforting arms. "Hi Mom, I wasn't expecting you so early." Emma stepped back from her mother, noting Carolynn's immaculate pantsuit, hairstyle and jewelry. Carolynn Dawson went nowhere, even the north woods, without looking as if she just stepped off the pages of a fashion magazine.

"Looks like we got here just in time." Carolynn watched as Rhonda rushed from the kitchen with a large tray laden with sandwiches and glasses of iced tea. "Ed, why don't you go on to the house and unload the luggage while I give Emma a hand."

"Aren't you hungry? Wouldn't you like some lunch first?"

"Naw, we stopped and had breakfast on the way." Ed patted her shoulder reassuringly. "Let me just say hello to a few of the guys, then I'll get out of your hair."

"I'll get the house key, my purse is back in the kitchen." Emma headed back, Carolynn close on her heels.

While Emma retrieved the key from her purse, Carolynn shed her white linen jacket and covered her blouse with one of Emma's aprons.

"Where do you need me to start, Rhonda?" she asked, not wasting any time. Rhonda shot her a grateful look and was giving instructions as Emma headed back out to the dinning room, key in hand.

Ed waved to his old friends as he made his way toward the door, Emma at his side. He slung a fatherly arm over her shoulders as they picked their way through the crowded parking lot to the Dawson's luxury car parked along the curb of Main Street. He gave his daughter a quick squeeze.

"So, baby, how are you, *really*?"

For a moment Emma allowed herself to lay her head on her father's shoulder, feeling safe and loved. Oh, to be a child again and have Daddy make everything all right. But she was grown and she knew her Heavenly Father was looking after her. She had to stop making people think she was so weak. Like Tyler. She straighten away from Ed with a small sigh.

"Oh Dad, it all seems like some horrible, bad dream. Today, out here in the sunshine, I find it hard to believe the last few days even happened at all." Emma shook her head and leaned against the side of her father's car.

"Does Nate have any idea at all who might be responsible?"

"No. They sent the notes to the State Police to be checked for fingerprints, but other than that, there aren't any leads yet." Emma's gaze drifted away. Over her father's shoulder she could see the trees that hid the Thunder Bay river and she thought of Adam Pearson. "Maybe it will all stop now that you're here."

"Maybe. That's something we can pray for." Ed patted her shoulder and reached to open the car door. "You know it will be nearly impossible for anyone to get past your mother," he said with a sardonic smile. "And if the person does keep trying, sooner or later he'll get caught."

"Yeah, I know, I just hope he doesn't try again. I want it all to go away."

"I know you do, baby, I know you do. But remember, God has a reason for all the trials we go through. There's something He wants you to learn from all this. You just need to ask Him to show you what it is." Ed slid behind the wheel of the car, leaving Emma to mull over his words.

The afternoon crowd finally thinned out and Emma was able to sit down with her mother at a corner table, dewy glasses of iced tea between them.

"Whew, I had forgotten what it was like to deal with the lunch time rush! No wonder you stay so slim." Carolynn pushed a stray curl of graying blond hair off her forehead and took a refreshing sip of her tea.

"Wait until this weekend when everyone is in town for the parade and everything. It's going to be complete chaos then. You ain't seen nothin' yet." Emma smiled across the table at her mother, thankful to have her parents here, feeling more relaxed already.

"I had sort of hoped that Milt and Mabel's nephew would come in for lunch. I'm curious to meet him. How is he doing now?"

Emma went still. She recalled all too clearly her mother's quick opinion of Tyler and his mental state. What could she say that wouldn't give away her growing feelings for him? Her mother knew her too well. She chose her words carefully.

"He seems to be doing very well." We're just friends, she said to herself, he's leaving at the end of the summer. "Actually, I have some good news.

Tyler's giving his life back to the Lord. He's been through some real tough times."

"Because of that accident Mabel mentioned?"

"Yes. It was really horrible." Emma gave her mother an abbreviated version of what Tyler had told her, leaving out the incident on County Road 487 which had unleashed all of Tyler's guilt and hurt.

"So see Mom, you had it all wrong when you told me he was mentally unbalanced!"

"I was just being cautious dear, that's all," Carolynn said with a small smile. "It's a mother's natural instinct to protect her child. That's why I'm glad we're here now."

Both women grew serious at the mention of the real reason why Carolynn and Ed had come to town. Emma wished she didn't have to have these constant reminders of the danger that was lurking somewhere in the beautiful woods she had grown up loving and feeling secure in.

"I know, Mom. I'm thankful you're here." Emma gave her mother's hands a hard squeeze as they lay on the table. "I appreciate all the help in the kitchen, too. Maybe I made up that stuff about the vandalism just to get you here so I could have some relief!" She laughed, trying to lighten the dark mood that had settled over them. The attempt fell flat.

"I wish it were only that Emma, I really do. But something, I don't know, I can't put my finger on it, but something inside me seems unsettled. I fear there's more to come."

Emma's heart sank like a lead weight. More to come? She had hoped her parent's arrival would bring peace, not warnings of more to fear.

With three sharing the burden, the clean up at the end of the day was done in record time. Emma found it a relief to close up shop and head home, her mother at her side. When they arrived they found Ed out on the back patio with steaks on the grill sending up a wonderful aroma into the still summer air.

"I figured you girls were going to be hungry and worn out after dealing with that crowd all day," Ed explained when Emma's amazed eyes met his. She gave him a grateful hug then turned to admire the patio table set with china and linen. Her parents never ceased to amaze her. She sat down in a lawn chair and reached to pour herself some lemonade from the pitcher on the table.

"This is really nice, Dad." Emma smiled up at him from her chair. "It's a real treat to come home and not have to think about cooking for a change."

"Your father always was handy with the grill." Carolynn seated herself at the patio table and helped herself to lemonade. She toed out of her pumps and put her feet up on the opposite chair, wiggling her toes in relief. "All those years we lived up here, the house filled with people every summer, there was nothing your dad liked more than showing off his expertise with whatever we had handy in the freezer at the moment. But fresh caught fish, that was his favorite, wasn't it dear?"

"Yes ma'am, nothing better than fresh caught bass cooked on the grill." Ed smacked his lips and turned the steaks.

"Speaking of the old place, how is it looking these days, Emma?" Carolynn asked. "I'm hoping to drive out there and take a look while we're here."

"It's looking great. The Craigs remind me a lot of how it was when we lived there, company all summer long and then deer hunters in the fall and snowmobilers all winter. But they love it."

"Maybe we could go after dinner and then stop in at Milt and Mabel's and see what their nephew's done with the cabin. I'm anxious to meet him."

Emma hesitated. She had vowed just last night to keep her distance from him. Prove to them both that she didn't need him. The more she had thought of it the worse it had seemed in her own eyes, her showing up on his doorstep at every opportunity. As if she were chasing him. What could she tell her parents that would sound like a plausible reason not to go? Emma glanced at her mother who was looking at her with narrow-eyed curiosity. Whatever excuse she gave, her mother would read the truth into it. She had that ability.

"Sure, we can do that," she finally agreed. "I'm sure Tyler will be happy to meet you and show you what he's done to the cabin." Her fickle heart betrayed her good intentions, beating with joy at the thought of seeing Tyler again.

The sun was beginning its slow descent into the west when Tyler carried a blanket from the cabin to the shady spot in the yard. He spread the blanket on the ground and laid down on his back, enjoying the cooling temperatures. He stretched contentedly and gazed up through the lattice of leaves to the clear blue sky, just now taking on tinges of purple in the gathering dusk.

Just last night Emma had sat in this exact spot. The memory came unbidden to his mind before Tyler could stop it. He didn't want to think of her. So why had pictures of her sitting in the canoe been floating across his mind all day? Why had dreams of her awakened him during the night with the urge to reach across the bed and pull her to him? Tyler's sigh blended with the breeze that rattled the leaves above him. What he was feeling for Emma was a far cry from friendship. How was he going to fight it for the rest of the summer?

Maybe he shouldn't stay. He had until Labor Day before he was expected back at work, but he was feeling better already. Tyler considered his job. How would it feel to be back on call? An involuntary shiver passed over his sweaty skin. If he had to get back into his rescue truck today, he doubted he'd be able to do it. Faced with an emergency situation, he would most likely fall apart like he did when he almost hit that little girl on the bike.

If it was the Lord's will, He would make Tyler able. Emma's voice seemed to echo through the whispering leaves. That's what Tyler wanted, more than anything. Even more than he wanted a life with Emma? Tyler shied away from the question. He loved his job. Eventually he would have to go back to work. Whatever he was feeling for Emma, it was just one more obstacle to get over on his road to full recovery. Maybe he wouldn't need the whole summer.

Tyler's eyes drifted closed and he concentrated on the cooling breeze blowing over him, drying the sweat from his day's work. He tried to picture his apartment, his co-workers. Tried to picture himself back on the job. The images refused to come into focus. All he could see behind his closed eyes was Emma's face with her heart-stopping smile and cupid's bow lips, perfect for kissing. Tyler forced his eyes back open, trying to dispel the picture in his mind, of Emma in his arms. Maybe what he needed was a swim in the cold lake.

Before he could get up, a white, luxury model car pulled into the drive, stopping behind his truck. Puzzled by the unfamiliar car and driver, Tyler slowly got to his feet. The bottom dropped out of his stomach as the object of his recent daydreams climbed from the car.

"Hi Tyler." Emma's smile was shy, lacking some of its normal radiance. Tyler still felt its impact across the stretch of yard. "I hope you don't mind, but my parents wanted to come and meet you and see the cabin."

An older, nicely dressed couple got out of the car as Tyler made his way across the tall grass. Emma's parents were here, his job as protector truly was over. His promise to Aunt Mabel no longer held him. As Emma approached, a lovely blond woman by her side, Tyler steeled himself against the emotions boiling within him.

"This is my dad, Ed, and my mom, Carolynn," Emma made the introductions.

Tyler shook hands with both of them, noticing

how they looked him up and down as if assessing him inch by inch. Were his feelings for Emma written clearly on his face? Tyler wondered.

"It's nice to meet you," Tyler said, averting his eyes from Emma, worried that his thoughts would show too clearly. "My aunt and uncle speak very highly of you both."

"I can honestly same the same thing about you, Tyler," Carolynn said, still looking him over closely. "Your Aunt Mabel is extremely fond of you. We can't wait to see what you've done to the place." Carolynn turned toward the cabin and Tyler was relieved to be released from her searching gaze. "It looks a hundred percent better already. Milt will be so pleased."

"I hope so, I'm really grateful to them for letting me use the place for the summer. Fixing it up has been good…therapy." He hesitated slightly over the word as Carolynn directed another probing look his way. Tyler mentally squirmed, feeling as if she were trying to read his mind.

"What all have you gotten done so far?" Ed moved toward the cabin and Tyler automatically fell into step beside him, explaining the repairs he had finished. Every nerve in his body was aware of Emma's presence behind him. Tyler fought the urge to reach back and take her hand, feel her warmth spread through him. They were only friends, he thought to himself sarcastically.

As they entered the cabin, Tyler walked across to switch on a small lamp that was now situated in the living room.

"Everything looks great." Ed walked about the small room, stopping to turn on the newly installed tap at the kitchen sink. "It must have taken a lot of work to get the plumbing working."

"Not too bad. Uncle Milt had gotten a start and most of the main supplies were already here, just waiting, like they were frozen in time. I was able to get a book on how to install the toilet and sink."

"So the bathroom is now in working order? Mabel will be so happy about that," Carolynn interjected. "Maybe they'll start using the place now that she doesn't have to fool with that path bath anymore. She enjoyed roughing it in her younger days, but you know how it is when you get older." Her quick laugh filled the room, reminding Tyler of Emma's lilting giggle. She patted Tyler's arm as she walked around the cramped space of the living room. "I can't wait to tell her everything you've done to the place, she's going to be so thrilled! It really seems like a miracle."

A miracle. Yes, the Lord had performed a couple of those since Tyler's arrival. He prayed the Lord would perform another and remove this growing love for Emma from his heart. Tyler scratched the bridge of his nose self-consciously.

"I don't know how miraculous it was. Just a lot of hard work and elbow grease. I hope Uncle Milt and Aunt Mabel will be able to get some use out of the place now." He risked a glance at Emma, standing by the door. She gave him a half-hearted smile and Tyler could feel the deep chasm that had opened between them. He reminded himself that it was best this way.

"Um, Mom and Dad, it's getting late," Emma finally spoke. "I need to be at the shop bright and early, and I'm sure Tyler is tired from his hard day of work. We probably should go."

"You're right. We'd better get you home." Carolynn joined Emma at the door, casting a quizzical look between Emma and Tyler. "It was nice meeting you, Tyler, I hope we see you again while we're in town."

Ed held out a hand and shook Tyler's firmly.

"Good meeting you. You've done a great job on the place."

Tyler merely nodded and watched them from the porch as they went through the screen door and out to their car. He waved a hand in farewell as the car turned around and headed down the drive. Tyler's heart felt as if it were being ripped in two as he watched Emma's sad profile disappear. It really is for the best, he told himself again. But best for who was a question he wasn't able to answer.

CHAPTER FIFTEEN

"*Emma, what are you doing here?*" *Emma stood before the door of the cabin, Tyler behind the screen. "Go away, you shouldn't be here, it's not safe." Emma tried to open the door but Tyler held it firmly closed.*

"What's going on in there?"

"Just go away!" Tyler yelled. "I don't want you here. I'm going home soon, far away from you and all this mess. No one will ever know…"

"Tyler, what are you saying? What are you doing in there? You didn't leave those flowers did you? You didn't threaten me. Tell me it's not true!! Tell me…"

With a start Emma sat bolt up-right in bed, her heart galloping like a runaway horse. What a strange, horrible dream! Why had her subconscious conjured up such a dreadful thing? She put a hand to her chest, feeling the rapid drumbeat of her heart. Tyler wasn't responsible for the vandalism, he hadn't left those dead roses, he *hadn't*! She knew it in the deepest part of her being.

A soft breeze blew through the open window, making the white Pricilla curtains billow slightly. Emma took a deep breath, trying to steady her nerves and slow the blood that was racing through her veins. Another calming breath. What was that smell? It smelled like smoke. A glance at her night-stand showed the clock to read 2:30 a.m. No one would be barbecuing at this hour. Had her father forgotten to turn off the grill?

Slowly Emma slid out of bed. With only the glow of the clock to guide her she made her way to the window and held back the curtain. The smell of smoke was heavier now and with the next gust of wind, she saw why.

"Daddy!! Daddy!!" Emma rushed for her bedroom door, flung it open and raced down the short hallway. She pounded on the door of the guest room. "Daddy, the garage is on fire!"

Without waiting for her parents to leave the room she rushed down the stairs and through the living room to the kitchen. She grabbed up the phone from the wall and punched in 9-1-1. Her parents were coming down the stairs, robes billowing behind them just as the dispatcher came on the line. In a rushed, panicked voice Emma told the dispatcher about the flames shooting out of her garage. Ed opened the back door and all three of them stood, momentarily transfixed by the vision that met their eyes. Emma's carriage house was quickly being engulfed in flames, and its proximity to the house meant the fire could spread at any moment.

"Come on, we need to get out of here!" Ed pushed Carolynn toward the front door. "Emma, tell them we have to get out of the house!"

Shaking with fear, Emma relayed the facts to the dispatcher, confirmed her address and hung up the phone. But she couldn't leave. Her eyes were drawn to the catastrophe taking place right outside her back door. Flames licked the walls of the garage. Through the small windows she could see the eerie glow that was devouring all her precious possessions. She couldn't keep herself from taking a small step toward the back door. Ed grabbed her arm.

"We need to get out of here Emma. With this wind, the flames could jump right to the house!" Mercilessly he drug her through the living room to the front porch just as the sirens of the fire engines broke the silence of the night.

A couple of hours later Emma sat huddled on the couch, a soft blanket around her shoulders. Involuntary shivers periodically shook her small frame. Her mother sat close beside her, her father perched on the opposite side, siting on the arm of the sofa. Emma shielded her eyes with a delicate hand. Her garage was a ruin. Not burned to the ground, but everything inside was a total loss and the structure would have to be re-built. She had insurance and, in time, could replace both the garage and the contents. But insurance money could never buy back the peace of mind and the trust that she had lost.

There was no denying it now. Someone was out to hurt her. Someone hated her enough to cause permanent damage to her property and endanger not only her life but her parents as well. Who? Adam Pearson was the only name that came to mind. But why? She couldn't think of one possible reason that Adam would have to hate her. She hardly even knew he existed. They hadn't ever exchanged more than a few words over the whole course of his life. It didn't make any sense. But if it wasn't Adam, it suddenly struck Emma, if he wasn't responsible, he just might know who was.

Suddenly her dream came back to her. Tyler! In the nightmare he was threatening her, alluding that he was to blame for everything that had happened. No! It was just a dream, only a dream. Tyler couldn't possibly have done any of this. She was sure the State Police would prove he hadn't written the note. Tyler would never hurt her.

Wouldn't he? A voice seemed to mock her. How could she be so sure? She didn't know him that well, didn't know him at all, she had to admit to herself. Even her own mother had warned her to be careful, that he was possibly mental. Nate Sweeney himself suspected him.

As if conjured up by her thoughts, the officer came in the back door and made his way through the kitchen to the living room. He was dressed in blue jeans and T-shirt, his dark hair rumpled, having obviously been called out of bed. His blue eyes held nothing but empathy as he hunkered down in front of her.

"How ya doing, Emmy?"

Emma lowered the hand that had shielded her eyes and looked from the gun in Nate's shoulder holster straight into his vivid blue eyes that held so much concern. Why, oh why couldn't she feel something for Nate besides friendship? She knew how he felt about her. She would be safe with him. No one would be able to hurt her if she allowed herself to become involved with him. As Nate Sweeney's wife, she would be protected. Her eyes fell once more on his gun.

The beloved of the Lord shall dwell in safety by Him.

It was as if someone whispered the words in her ear. Another shiver passed over her skin, but this time it was as if the Holy Spirit passed over her and Emma took strength from it. She didn't need a man to keep her safe. The Lord was with her. He had woke her up just in time to see the fire in the garage, they were all okay. She would not doubt and she would not allow herself to turn to Nate for comfort.

"The guys have the fire out. They're just hanging around out there for awhile longer, making sure there aren't any hot spots. Good thing you live so close to the fire station, with this wind there's no telling what could have…" he let his words trail off but Emma knew what he did not say. She could have lost her house, possibly her life. He cleared his throat.

"We found this out on the patio table, weighted down with a rock. It's obvious that whoever set the fire, left it as a warning, just like before."

Nate held out a small square of white paper. The paper and the block printing looked identical to the note that had been left in her car.

THEY CAN'T PROTECT YOU EMMA

With a sharp intake of breath, Emma clutched

the blanket at her throat. It was as if the arsonist had crawled inside her mind and heard what she had been thinking.

"So, they don't think the fire was an accident?" she asked in a near whisper.

"They'll have to do a full investigation, but given the evidence so far, and what's been happening in the past week, no, we're pretty sure it wasn't an accident. Do you have any idea Emma, any at all, who might be responsible. If you have any suspicions, it's imperative that you tell me. Did you see anything, hear anything?"

"Oh for heaven's sake Nate, we were in bed!" Carolynn's imperious voice cut into his questions.

"I have to ask, Mrs. Dawson, it's police procedure."

"Pish-posh," Carolynn began to dismiss the deputy but Emma took her mother's hand and squeezed it.

"It's okay, Mom. Nate has a job to do and he's doing it."

Emma proceeded to explain what they had done the previous evening, going over their every move as dispassionately as she could. A picture of Adam Pearson seemed to be lodged in her mind, but Emma didn't mention it. She knew she should tell Nate. He had said "any suspicions" but she just couldn't bring herself to say the words. After all, she didn't have any *evidence* that Adam had done anything wrong. He was obviously a very troubled boy. What would it do to him if he was innocent and Emma put the cops on his tail? What would it do to Doreen?

Emma knew her reasons went deeper than that. As long as she didn't say anything, didn't put voice to her suspicions, then she could pretend this wasn't real. Somehow, saying it out loud, putting a possible name and a face to it made it seem so much more evil. Instead she skipped to the end of the story, how she had gone to bed and awakened to smell smoke.

When she was finished, Nate stood and stretched then took a small plastic bag from his jeans pocket. He carefully put the note inside.

"Have you heard anything from the State Police yet?" Emma asked quietly. "Did the other notes reveal anything?"

Nate shook his head.

"There weren't any prints. They've sent it on to an expert to analyze the handwriting and compare it to the sample."

"So Tyler's not completely off the hook?" A wisp of her nightmare floated before her eyes. She forced the vision away. It had only been a dream!

"What do you mean?" Carolynn asked suspiciously. "What has Tyler got to do with all of this?"

"Probably nothing." Nate shrugged a wide shoulder. "We just had to make sure, since he came to town at the exact time the vandalism started. He was a stranger to the town and therefore a suspect."

Emma's heart sank as she saw her mother's eyes narrow and knew the track her train of thought was going down.

"Hmm. And have you questioned him? Does he have an alibi?"

"Mother!" Emma jumped up, immediately ready

to come to Tyler's defense.

"Well, Emma, Nate's right." Carolynn looked at the deputy with new respect. "It is suspicious that all this started happening after Tyler arrived. Does he have an alibi?"

Nate slid a knowing look Emma's way.

"Not air tight, no. But Emma seems convinced the guy has no reason to threaten her." Carolynn's expression said Nate's answer was far from satisfactory. "We are investigating every lead, Mrs. Dawson. I will catch who's doing this. I can promise you that much."

"It's not Tyler," Emma said adamantly.

Her father rose from his perch on the arm of the sofa and put a protective arm around Emma's shoulders. Instinctively she leaned her head into his neck.

"You should probably try to get some rest, baby."

"What time is it anyway?" Emma peered at the clock on the mantle.

"Just about five."

"Five! I have to get dressed and get to the shop!"

"You can't be serious honey," Carolynn said in disbelief. "You can't go in today. Leave the shop closed, everyone will understand."

"No Mom, I won't do that. It's my business, my life. I won't let this, this *terrorist* ruin everything! He can threaten me all he wants, I'm not giving in to his evilness."

"But it's not safe. Nate, tell her it's not safe!" Carolynn turned pleading eyes on the deputy.

"I don't know Emma, I agree with your mother. This person is serious now. I don't like the thought of you exposing yourself to so much danger. Until we catch this creep, or get you more protection, it might be best if you leave the shop closed."

"I will not be a prisoner." Emma pulled away from her father's arm and straightened herself. "What is that song we used to sing in church, Mom? Be not afraid, I go before you always, come, follow me, and I will give you rest." Emma's clear voice sang the hymn without wavering. "I am not going to live in fear. And whoever is doing this, he's after me, for whatever warped reason that might be. I doubt he'll attack me in my own restaurant, or burn down a building full of people. I am going to work."

CHAPTER SIXTEEN

A fire in the early morning hours was big news in a small town. The Spot of Tea was filled to capacity most of the day. Some were tourists in the area for the holiday, but most were curious regulars, hungry for details of the latest crime. After answering questions all morning, Emma finally had all her tired mind could take and retreated to the kitchen to prepare orders while her mother and Rhonda handled the front.

The locals all showed unquestionable concern for Emma. She appreciated the words of comfort, but to her dismay found herself suspicious of every-one around her. Was it possible that one of these people, someone she had known all her life, wanted to cause her harm? She couldn't believe it was true, *wouldn't* believe it.

"Whew, that was getting crazy out there!" Carolynn came into the kitchen and immediately went to Emma and began rubbing her back. "How are you holding up?"

"Okay, I guess." Emma glanced at the clock. "I'm not sure I'll be able to make it the whole day, no matter how determined I want to be."

"I know sweetie. If you want to close up early, the customers will understand. You've proved your point, but this is going to take its toll and you are going to have to give yourself a break and get some rest. Don't let yourself be so stubborn that you fall over from exhaustion."

"I won't Mom, and thank you." Emma turned and gave her mother a tight hug. "I don't know what I would have done if you and Daddy hadn't been here. You got here just in time."

The words brought back her mother's warning of the day before, her fear that there was more to come. Was the fire the "more" and would this be the last of it? Emma knew with certainty it wasn't.

"It's slowed way down now. Why don't you make yourself a cup of tea and we'll go sit for a little while. A short rest will do you good."

"That sounds like a good idea." Emma took cups and saucers from the cupboard and filled a tea pot with hot water. Moments later they were seated at the corner table.

"Emma, dear, I know you don't want me to pry. But I really want to understand. Why are you so sure that Tyler McGillis doesn't have anything to do with what's happened?"

"Oh Mom, do we have to discuss this now?" Emma dropped her head into her hands. She was so tired. How could she ever explain her feelings to her mother?

"Over the phone I got the distinct impression that something was going on between the two of you. But then last night you barely looked at each other. I'm your mother, Emma. I have a sixth sense about these things. I wish you would tell me what's really going on."

"Nothing's going on." Emma sighed and took a sip of her tea. It was time to come clean. In the last week she had become very adept at twisting the truth. If she was going to be honest, the best place to start was with her feelings for Tyler.

"You're right. There is something between us. I'm, I'm very attracted to him. I think I made a fool of myself, practically throwing myself at his feet. I'm embarrassed to even think about it now. He's shown nothing but concern for me. He's the one who told me I should drive to work, and then the next day my tires were slashed. When I told him what had happened, he was genuinely shocked and upset about it. It wasn't an act. I thought maybe there was a chance for us, beyond friendship, but he reminded me that he's only here for the summer. He has a job he loves back in the city and he doesn't want either one of us getting hurt. So." Emma finally met her mother's gaze across the table. "We've agreed to just be friends. I admit, I thought at first that maybe he was the one the Lord had planned for me. But I guess I was wrong. I do know that he's *not* the one threatening me."

Carolynn sat back in her chair and gave Emma an encouraging smile.

"Okay. You've convinced me. As for Tyler being

your Mr. Right, don't underestimate what the Lord can do. His arm is not too short. I know how stubborn you are, how determined when you set your mind to something. Don't harden your heart to what the Lord may have in store for you."

Emma looked skeptically at her mother. "That's funny advice, coming from someone who has been so suspicious of Tyler from the beginning."

"Just call it woman's intuition. And I trust your judgement. So, if Tyler isn't responsible for what's been happening, then who?"

Emma thought of Adam. She was coming clean, should she admit her suspicions about Adam, too? She hadn't seen him in days, so what was the point? Her doubts were probably misplaced.

"I don't know, Mom," Emma finally said. "I wish I did."

The two got up from the table and carried their tea cups back to the kitchen, Carolynn's countenance thoughtful.

"It's still slow," Carolynn observed. "Do you think you'll be okay to handle things for awhile? I've got an errand I really need to run, if you think you can spare me for an hour."

Surprised, Emma looked sharply at her mother. Carolynn's face gave nothing away. Emma shrugged and began assembling ingredients for sandwich fillings.

"Sure, I'll be okay. It's usually slow around this time and if things get real hairy again, I can always press Dad into playing waitress." Emma smiled for the first time that day.

"Great." Carolynn grabbed her handbag and went across the kitchen to press a gentle kiss onto Emma's cheek. "I'll be back soon, I promise."

"Be careful, Mom," Emma warned. "It probably isn't a good idea for you to be running around town alone either."

"Oh pish-posh." Carolynn smiled and waved an elegant hand. "I'll be perfectly safe sweetie. You don't have to worry about me a bit." With that she slipped from the kitchen door out into the parking lot, Emma's quizzical gaze following her the whole way.

Tyler heard the sound of a slamming car door and stifled the curse that nearly tumbled from his lips. If he had come to the north woods to be alone then he had obviously come to the wrong place.

"Hellooo!" Tyler heard someone call out. "Anybody home?"

He made his way to the screened in porch, surprised to see Emma's mother standing at the door.

"Mrs. Dawson." Tyler nodded at her through the screen. "I wasn't expecting to see you out here today. Come on in." He unlatched the door and pushed it open for her.

"Yes, well," Carolynn's normal eloquence seemed to desert her as she followed him into the cabin. "There was some excitement in town last night, and since you don't have a phone, I thought I should be the one to come out and tell you about it. Unless of course, Nate Sweeney has already been out to question you."

"I haven't seen Sweeney," Tyler said, his blood

running cold as he slowly turned to face Emma's mother. "What's happened?"

"He hasn't been here? I had heard you might be a suspect."

Tyler felt her penetrating gaze, knew she was sizing him up and drawing her own conclusions. He stood still under her perusal, clenching his fists in frustration.

"What kind of excitement, Mrs. Dawson?" he asked again.

She seemed to reach her conclusion as she finally answered. "Well you see, someone set fire to Emma's garage."

"What?!" He dropped into a kitchen chair, stunned. "Is Emma okay?" His piercing gaze searched her face. If Emma was hurt, her mother wouldn't be here now. Relieved, he managed to ask, "What happened?"

"I can't say exactly." Carolynn sat down in the opposite chair and folded her hands on the table top. "Emma woke up in the middle of the night and smelled smoke. When she looked outside, the garage was on fire. With the wind, we were very worried the fire would jump to the house. Thankfully the fire department is very close and they got there quickly, so only the garage and the contents were lost."

"Oh my Lord." Tyler ran his hands through his hair and dug his fingers into his scalp, trying to help the reality sink in. Emma could have died. She would have been lost to him forever. "They think it was arson for sure?"

"Well, there was another note."

Tyler went still, his jaw clenched in anger. "What did it say?" he finally managed to ask.

"It said 'they can't protect you Emma,' written just like the others, at least Nate and Emma said it was the same. That's why I thought Nate might have come out and asked you about it. He said you don't have an air-tight alibi for the other incidents."

"I'm not the one threatening your daughter, Mrs. Dawson. I give you my word. I swear on this Bible right here." Tyler pulled the book that was laying open on the table in front of him.

"Emma said the same thing. I admit, I wondered." Her gold flecked eyes, so similar to her daughter's, searched Tyler's face once more. "I believe you both, which is why I'm here."

"I don't understand." Tyler sat back in the chair, crossing his arms over his chest.

"I feel the danger is far from over. And Emma, well, you'd have to know my daughter to understand. She's very stubborn. Gets it from her mother, Ed says." Carolynn laughed. "Believe it or not, she insisted on opening the shop today, even though both Nate and I tried to discouraged her."

Tyler watched and waited as he fought mental images of Emma burning up in a fire. As a member of Toledo's fire and rescue unit, he'd seen more than his fair share of burn victims. It was torture thinking that Emma had nearly suffered the same fate.

"The truth is, I want to ask a favor of you," Carolynn finally came to her point. "I know I don't have any right to ask anything of you. You don't know me, but Emma considers you a friend. She trusts you and she's going to need someone to look out for her in the next couple of days. There will be hundreds of people in town for the holiday. Whoever is looking to hurt Emma, he picked the perfect time to try and do it. There will be people milling around everywhere and she'll be very vulnerable. Nate and the other deputies will have their eyes and ears open, but they're going to have their hands full with all the other normal holiday disasters. They can't give one-hundred percent of their resources to watching Emma. So, that leaves you."

Tyler dropped his arms and stared at the woman seated across from him.

"You want me to be Emma's bodyguard?"

Carolynn smiled and Tyler realized if Emma aged as gracefully as her mother, she was going to be even more beautiful in the future. But he wouldn't be around to see it.

"A bodyguard is a wonderful idea, but I just told you, Emma is stubborn. I've never known a girl more determined to do things her own way. If she thinks we've arranged for you to guard her, she'll probably do everything in her power to slip through your fingers. We have to be much more subtle than that."

"Go on, I'm listening."

"Since you're a tourist, you can blend in easy enough with the crowds in town. Well, maybe not that easy." She looked Tyler up and down, admiration in her eyes. Tyler felt himself blushing and Carolynn laughed.

"I'm asking that you keep an eye on her, even if it's from a distance. Or just be hanging around.

That's not so unusual for the Fourth of July. And Emma did say you were friends." Her knowing eyes were assessing him again and Tyler squirmed. "Will you do it, Tyler? I know you came up here for your own reasons, and if you say no, I'll understand."

A war began in Tyler's head. Getting close to Emma Dawson for whatever reason was dangerous business, and he didn't mean physical. But the thought of any harm coming to her sent a stab of fear piercing through him. He didn't have to get close to her. He could just watch from a distance. That should be safe enough. A few days, that was all. And then the sooner he got out of here and headed back to Toledo, the better. Decision made, he sat up straighter and nodded, one slow nod.

"Okay, I'll do it."

"Oh, thank you!" Carolynn clapped her hands together and got up. "I will be in your debt forever. Now, I've got to go. I promised Emma I would be back to the shop within an hour."

Tyler watched as Carolynn hurried out the door and back to her car. What in the world had he done? He had just made another promise that he wasn't sure he could keep. But the thought of someone trying to hurt Emma, possibly even kill her, brought rage to a full boil inside of him. She was everything that was good, and sweet, and innocent. He closed his eyes and saw her brilliant smile, heard her musical laughter. Then he saw a fire, could see in his mind's eye how closely the fire had come to her home, how easily she could have been killed. The image made him physically sick. He tried to imagine his life now, without Emma in it, and all color faded from his surroundings.

What was he going to do? Last night he had felt certain that staying away from Emma was for the best. Now he could think of anything but staying away from her. He felt consumed with the need to protect her.

Immediately doubts assailed him. Who was he to think he could protect Emma? He who had taken an oath to serve and protect and instead had killed an innocent child. He wasn't qualified to protect anyone. Tyler's shoulders slumped as he rested his elbows on the table, dropping his face into his hands. His fingers played over the ridge of scar. He was fooling himself, and Emma's mother, thinking he could keep Emma safe. He opened his eyes and his gaze fell on the Bible laying open on the table. Maybe he wasn't qualified to be Emma's protector, but now he knew Someone who was more than able. Tyler got down on his knees then and there, folded his hands and bowed his head.

Somehow Emma made it through the day. She had no idea how, only that the Lord gave her the strength required to make it until four o'clock. But she couldn't help be relieved when the clock hit four and the last customer finally left. Emma didn't think she could answer one more question or accept one more piece of well meant advice. She just wanted to go home and go to bed.

The thought sent a chill up her spine. She was bone tired but the thought of going back to her house, trying to sleep in her bed, knowing someone was watching her, she didn't think she could do it. Fear swept through her, so strong and fierce she was momentarily paralyzed.

Someone was trying to *kill* her! The reality settled over her like a heavy, wet blanket, smothering her. Spray paint and slashed tires, even the dead roses with their threatening message, had been easy enough to dismiss as pranks. But fire. She couldn't deny the truth any longer. Someone wanted her dead. And if not dead, then seriously hurt. Why? What had she done?

Tired beyond reason, Emma didn't know where to turn. A picture of Adam flashed through her mind. What should she do with what little knowledge she had? She didn't have any real facts, just some suspicions and vague feelings. Certainly not any evidence. If she went to Nate now he would go off half-cocked and possibly cause untold damage to a family already on the brink. There was no one she could go to, no one dispassionate enough to listen and be rational about the situation. Everyone she knew was too emotionally involved. They would all assume the worst.

Tyler wouldn't. The words popped into her mind. Tyler wasn't emotionally involved. He didn't know the Pearsons or anyone else in this town, so he wouldn't have any preconceived notions about them or jump to any conclusions. She could tell him what she knew in a hypothetical way. He wouldn't have to know who she was talking about.

Only problem, she was supposed to keep her

distance from him. No more playing damsel in distress and throwing herself at his feet. She had made a bad enough impression on him already. Who else could she trust? Tyler was the only one she could think of who wasn't emotionally involved. He wouldn't go off wanting to arrest someone without real evidence. She trusted his opinion, and they were friends. Emma was still trying to rationalize her need to see Tyler when her mother entered the kitchen.

"Everything's all taken care of in the dining room," Carolynn stated. Emma noticed a new bounce in her mother's step and what was that light shining in her mother's eyes? If Emma didn't know better, she would say her mother was up to no good.

"The dishes are finished but I really should get some things started for tomorrow. Normally I stay and prepare as much as I can ahead of time, and the next couple of days are going to be hectic with the holiday." Emma put a tired hand to her forehead as she sank onto a high stool.

"Oh pish-posh." Carolynn stopped next to Emma, letting her exhausted daughter wilt into her side. "You are going home and going to bed. We are both exhausted and won't be good to anyone if we don't get some rest. Tomorrow will take care of itself. If you run out of muffins, then you'll just have to close your doors. I'm sure your customers will understand."

"Maybe so, but this is the best time of year for my business. I can't afford to lose the money. Come November this town will be practically empty except for hunters and snowmobilers. I have to have a good summer to make it through the winter."

"Hey." Carolynn tilted Emma's chin up. "Who isn't trusting in the Lord now, huh? He will see you through, physically and financially. Right?"

"Right," Emma sighed as she said the word.

"Come on, let's get you home. A little sleep will do wonders for you. After you've gotten some rest, things won't look so bleak."

CHAPTER SEVENTEEN

Emma lay on her bed, exhausted but unable to sleep. The smell of smoke still hung heavy in the air. She wished she had invested in central air conditioning. The stinging, acrid odor permeated everything, making it impossible for her to sleep. The fear crept back in. Her house was no longer a safe haven. Was the person watching the house right now? Did he know they were all here, sleeping, or trying to? Was he just waiting to light another match?

Emma sat bolt upright, her heart pounding. She looked toward the window. Don't be ridiculous, she told herself. It was still broad daylight. And one of the deputies was hanging around outside somewhere. She was perfectly safe, so why didn't she *feel* it? She had thought for sure with her parents here everything would go back to normal, her life would get back on an even keel. She almost laughed out loud. Her life had been off kilter since Tyler McGillis had walked into the Spot of Tea.

Tyler. A heavy sigh escaped her as she slid out of bed and went to the window. As if being physically threatened wasn't enough to throw her life into chaos, she had to be emotionally threatened, too. Tyler had tried to warn her, but he was too late. When he left he would carry home the scars on his body, but he would leave behind a giant scar on her heart. She would just have to avoid him for the rest of the summer, Emma decided. Distance was the key. She didn't have to see him, and in a couple of months, he'd be gone. Case solved. At least one case.

Her sad hazel eyes drank in the sight of her ruined garage. The blackened timbers reached their broken arms up toward the pristine sky. Had Adam done that? Had he destroyed her possessions, and her piece of mind, and come close to burning her and her parents alive? And what about Doreen? Emma remembered the woman's battered and bruised face. If Adam had done that, then her life could be in danger, too. She had to talk to Tyler. The vision of Adam was haunting her, and if she didn't talk to someone she was going to go crazy.

Emma tossed aside her decision to keep her distance from Tyler and quietly slipped into shorts and a T-shirt. Soundlessly she opened her bedroom door, checking the hallway and listening for sounds from her parents' room. She prayed they were sleeping as she made her way stealthily down the stairs. If she got caught trying to sneak out, she would have to make some sort of excuse and what would she be able to say that would make any sense?

One step at a time, Emma crept slowly down the stairs, listening for any sounds in the house. She felt a giggle rise in her throat. This was ridiculous. She felt like a criminal in her own home, creeping down the stairs like a thief! She stifled the laughter as she remembered the seriousness of her situation. Her life was at stake.

Sobered, she made it down the stairs and to the front door. Did it squeak when opened? Emma thought hard, her sleep starved brain fuzzy. Think, think, think. Did it click, squeak, groan? She couldn't remember. She turned the brass knob and the door swung open on silent hinges. Emma expelled the breath she had been holding, grabbed her purse from the pie crust table by the door, and eased out onto the porch. Free at last she ran to her car, now parked at the curb, and headed toward Tyler. The one place her heart knew she would be truly safe.

Fresh caught fish sizzled over the fire as Tyler hunkered down beside the grill. He looked up as Emma's car pulled into the drive and stopped behind his truck. His heart went completely still as he met her tired gaze across the yard. Slowly Emma got out of the car and walked toward him. Even in denim shorts and a plain white T-shirt, Tyler thought she was the most beautiful thing he had ever seen. Her hair was down, flying loose in the breeze. It was long and full of natural wave, hair a man instinctively wanted to put his hands into.

Taking his mind off her physical attributes, Tyler looked up into her eyes, saw the dark circles under them, the lines of worry creasing the corners.

"Hey." She stopped next to the fire.

"Hey yourself." Tyler moved the fish to the side of the grill, away from the heat of the coals and slowly stood.

"Been fishing again, I see." Emma tried to smile, but it didn't quite reach her eyes.

"Yeah, I got up early and tried my hand. Thought I might have better luck." Tyler hated reminding them both of their last trip out on the lake together. When they had agreed to just be friends. "I hear you got up pretty early yourself this morning."

"Oh yeah? Where'd you hear that?"

"A little bird told me." Tyler realized his mistake. He didn't want Emma to know about his conversation with her mother. He scratched the bridge of his nose nervously. "You know how news spreads in a small town, like..." Tyler barely caught himself before he made another huge blunder. "Like butter on hot toast."

"That's not what you were going to say, you were going to say wild fire." The sadness and emptiness in Emma's eyes nearly broke Tyler's heart. "So, you must have been in town today huh, to hear the news."

"I heard alright." Tyler didn't correct her assumption of where he heard it. "I'm really glad you weren't hurt, Em." Tyler busied himself once more with the fish, not wanting Emma to see just how true his words were.

"My guardian angel must have nudged my shoulder and woke me up I guess. I have to be thankful for that."

Tyler eased the fish onto a plate and stood up.

"Want to join me for dinner? There's plenty for two." He held his breath, praying she would accept his invitation, yet scared to death she would. He had promised to watch out for her, but it was supposed to be from a distance. Getting this close was decidedly dangerous, perhaps not for her, but definitely for him.

Emma looked at him with those tired eyes. Tyler could see the change in her. A part of her innocence had been lost forever. He knew how that felt and silently raged at the person who had taken something from Emma that could never be replaced.

"Come on." Tyler couldn't resist putting his arm around her slumped shoulders. "Come and eat with me and tell me what brought you out here. I have a feeling it wasn't my cooking." A small giggle escaped Emma and Tyler squeezed her shoulders in relief. She had been knocked down, but she was not destroyed. "That's my girl." He held the screen door open for her and followed her into the dim interior of the cabin.

Emma sat at the table and toyed with the fish and potatoes on her plate. She needed to find the right way to word her concerns to Tyler, but all her tired mind could think of was how good it had felt to have his arm around her. He had called her 'his girl.' The words sent a thrill through her, despite her exhaustion.

That's not why you're here, Emma reminded herself. She had to keep her thoughts on the problem at hand; Adam Pearson and the fact that he might be out to kill her.

"So." Tyler stretched his muscled arms above his head then crossed them over his broad chest. He sat back in his chair, staring intently at Emma. "Do you want to tell me what's on your mind?"

The pointed question took Emma by surprise, startling her fuzzy mind into coherence. 'You have a really nice chest,' seemed lodged in her brain. She shook her head to clear her thoughts. She certainly couldn't tell Tyler that her mind had a penchant for lingering on him and how he made her feel. Why was she here again? Oh yes, Adam and what *he* made her feel.

Emma looked deeply into Tyler's eyes. Could she really trust him? She looked back down at her plate, away from those green eyes that had seen too much. Emma was afraid they would see right to the core of her, see how weak and afraid she really was. See how her whole body and soul wanted to reach toward him, find comfort and safety in his arms. Emma sighed.

"You're right, there is a reason I'm here. There's something I wanted to talk over with you, you know, get your opinion about. It's just hard to find the right way to say it."

Emma pushed away from the table and got up. She was so tired, exhaustion was quickly taking over her body and mind. She needed to move around before she laid her head down and fell asleep right there in her supper. She moved to the living room, looking at each object Tyler had placed in the small space. How much different the cabin felt now than it had a week ago. There was a hominess about the place now. It felt cozy. Safe and secure. Would her own house ever feel the same way again?

Tyler stayed at the table. Emma felt his gaze following her around the room. She swung her arms, trying to get her blood to pump more quickly through her body and clear her thinking.

"What if," she finally started, "someone saw something, you know, slightly suspicious? What if they sort of felt something, just a feeling, an intuition, about someone? Should that person go to the police with these feelings?"

"You're talking about the person who's threatening you, aren't you?" Tyler was up out of his chair like a shot. Before Emma could blink he was standing in front of her, commanding her to look at him. "Do you know something, Emma? If you do, you have to tell Sweeney."

"No, no, no," Emma denied, turning her back on Tyler once more. She definitely couldn't think clearly with him standing over her like that, protectiveness emanating from every pore. "I didn't say I know anything. I'm just asking, hypothetically, what if someone *thought* they knew something. Not really even know, just feel. Oh! I'm not saying this right at all!"

Frustrated, Emma flopped onto the sofa and put her head in her hands. The couch sagged as Tyler sat down beside her. The touch on her chin surprised her into lifting her face as Tyler's strong hand turned her toward him. This time she couldn't turn away. Her skin seemed to burn where he held her with just a finger. His look seared straight to her soul.

"Emma, you need to be honest with me. This is your life we're talking about. Don't play games with me. If you know something, or someone else thinks they know something, then spit it out."

"That's just it, I don't know if I really know anything. Does that even make any sense?" Emma fell back against the cushions of the sofa, away from Tyler's touch which was doing unbelievable things to her insides, making it impossible to think with her already muddled brain. "It's just a suspicion I have. I've seen someone, you know, sort of watching me lately and I…"

"Who, who have you seen watching you, Emma?" Tyler turned to look her fully in the face.

Emma saw the dark storm clouds gathering in his eyes. Her heart did a double flip but she quickly tried to still it. As much as Tyler's reaction thrilled her, Emma had to remind herself that there was more at stake here than her own emotions. Mistakenly she had thought Tyler would be neutral. Now she could tell if she gave him a name, he would be out the door and at the sheriff's office in a heartbeat. As much as his desire to protect her melted her heart, she wouldn't do that to Doreen, or to Adam, not without more proof.

"I'm not going to tell you." Emma crossed her arms stubbornly and set her chin. "I came out here because I thought you would be able to discuss this rationally with me and look at it from every angle. I'm trying to tell you, it's just a feeling I have, that's all, I don't have any proof this person means me any harm. And it wouldn't help if I gave you a name anyway, you don't know any of the people in town. All you would do is go tell Nate and he'd go flying off, sirens screaming and possibly make a mess of an already messy situation just because he's in love with me!"

"Do you love him?"

"Huh?" Emma's bleary eyes looked up at Tyler. He was changing the subject and her exhausted mind couldn't quite make the same turn.

"I said, do you love Nate?"

Emma giggled, making Tyler smile. She grew serious once more and sighed.

"No, no I don't, which is really too bad, with him being a policeman and all."

Emma gave a huge yawn and tucked her feet up on the love seat. She lay her head on the padded armrest, suppressing the sudden desire to tell Tyler it was he she was falling in love with. What would he do with that bit of information? Head for the city just as quick as his truck would carry him, most likely. She had been nothing but trouble since they'd met. She closed her eyes and tried to bring her wandering mind back to the subject at hand without much success. What had they been talking about? Oh yes, Adam.

"Lordy, I am so tired. I can't even think," Emma's speech grew slow and slurred. "And don't worry about what I said about Adam, it's really nothing. He just needs a lot of prayer, that's all."

Tyler watched Emma fall asleep. He went still. What had she just said? Who was Adam? And what she had said about him needing a lot of prayer, why did that sound familiar? His mind refused to function properly, distracted by the soft form sleeping next to him. Tyler rose, removed Emma's shoes and stretched her legs out more comfortably on the love seat. He couldn't help but smile as she sighed contentedly and curled up on her side. Going to his room to get a blanket, Tyler grinned as his heart repeated over and over "she doesn't love Nate Sweeney, she doesn't love Nate Sweeney."

As he was tucking the blanket around Emma's sleeping form realization hit him like a sledgehammer. They had been at the park when Emma had seen a boy there. He distinctly remembered the look of fear that had passed briefly over her features when she had seen him. Tyler had asked her about it and all she had said was that he needed a lot of prayer. Was that the Adam she had mentioned as she fell asleep? Had he been watching Emma then, thinking of ways to hurt her? Obviously Emma had seen him more than once or she wouldn't be suspicious. Tyler couldn't help but think that Emma knew far more than she was letting on. Her mother had said she was stubborn, and Tyler was quickly learning for himself just how true that was. He just prayed that her stubbornness didn't lead to disaster.

Tyler thought of Nate Sweeney. As much as he disliked the cocky deputy, he couldn't help but wish there was a phone at the cabin so he could call and relay the information. Maybe the name Adam would ring a bell. Tyler looked out the front window. It was quickly growing dark and he couldn't take a chance of leaving Emma alone while he ran into town. It would just have to wait until tomorrow.

CHAPTER EIGHTEEN

A flash of bright light through the cabin's front window brought Tyler awake. He had fallen asleep in the recliner and now his gritty eyes squinted at the beam of light that pierced through the darkness outside. A door slammed, bringing Tyler completely awake. He jumped from the chair, looking down to see that Emma was still sound asleep on the couch. He hurried to the door and walked out onto the screened in porch.

"Who's there!"

"McGillis, is that you?" Nate Sweeney's voice cut across the dark yard.

"Awfully late for visiting, isn't it deputy?" Tyler said as Nate moved toward the cabin. He stopped at the screen door.

"Not a social call. I see Emma's car is here. We've been out looking for her. Her parents thought she disappeared." Tyler didn't miss the strain in the deputy's voice but he couldn't help but smile.

"She hasn't disappeared Sweeney, she's inside."

Nate's eyes narrowed. "And just what is Emma doing inside?"

"Come on in and ask her yourself." Tyler unlatched the door and held it open. "She's not tied up or anything, I swear. She fell asleep on my couch."

"There had better be a good explanation for this. We've got half the town looking for her. Her parents are sick to death with worry. We thought for sure she'd been kidnapped."

Tyler turned to the deputy as realization dawned. "Are you telling me that no one knew where she was?" He shook his head in frustration. "I had no idea she hadn't told anyone where she was going. She's going to be the death of someone yet. I just hope it isn't herself!"

Emma stirred at the sound of doors closing and voices murmuring. She stretched sleepily and sat up, trying to get her bearings. Where was she?

"Hey Emma, you've got a visitor."

Tyler stood at the door of the cabin, a uniformed figure by his side. Emma rubbed her eyes, trying to recall why she was here.

"I fell asleep on your sofa," she stated the obvious. Tyler smiled.

"Yes, you did." He came to stand over her, hands on lean hips. "Emma, did you not tell anyone you were coming out here to talk to me?"

Emma looked up guiltily.

"Well, no," she drew out the word. "Mom and

dad were asleep and I didn't want to wake them up, and I knew if I told anyone, they'd insist on coming with me because I'm in so much blasted danger."

Tyler lowered himself to sit beside her and put a warm arm around her shoulders.

"Sweetheart, do you have any idea how much trouble your stubborn nature causes? Half of Montmorency County is searching for you. They think you've been kidnapped."

"Oh no!" Emma's tired eyes finally focused on Nate, who crossed his arms over his chest. "Really?" Her troubled gaze begged him to tell her it wasn't true.

"I'm afraid so," Nate's accusing tone bit into her conscience. "I thought I had made it clear you weren't to go anywhere alone, or at least let people know where you were going."

"And I thought I'd made it clear that I wasn't going to do any such thing!" Emma voice sounded childish, even to her own ears.

Nate's knowing eyes rested on Emma, then on Tyler, lingering on the arm that was draped over her shoulders.

"I would ask what you were doing out here, but I think that's obvious enough," Nate sneered.

"Oh Nate, for Pete's sake, get your mind out of the gutter!" Emma jumped up, removing herself from Tyler's arm. "Not that it's any of your business, but I just came out here to talk to Tyler. That's it. If you'll remember correctly, I didn't get much sleep last night. I accidentally drifted off during our conversation."

"Whatever you say, Emmy. It's your story to tell.

Now that I know there's no *real* danger, I'd better get back and tell your parents. Someone needs to be thinking about how they feel." He stopped at the door and looked once more at Emma. She saw clearly the hurt in his eyes. "What are the townspeople going to say when they find out you've been out here half the night? You know how people gossip. They're going to assume all sorts of things about you and that isn't a very good Christian witness, is it?"

"Oh my goodness!" Emma looked at Tyler, stricken. "They're going to think we, you, that we…" She turned red at the thought. "But we didn't do anything, we, oh Lord!" She dropped her face into her hands. As if she didn't have enough to worry about, now her reputation and good standing in town were at stake, too.

"I'm sorry Tyler. I never thought." Now that was the most truthful thing she had said in a long time.

"Great going, Sweeney." Tyler stood and put his hands on Emma's shoulders. "Calm down, Em. We know the truth and God knows the truth. Don't worry about anything else."

"No one needs to know!" A light bulb went on in Emma's brain and she pulled away from Tyler once more. "I'll just drive home right now, no one will know I was here, except Nate, and you won't say anything, will you?" Her desperate eyes rested on the man in uniform. "I'll just go home and tell every-one I went for a drive, that I needed to get away. That's it. No one will be the wiser."

"I'm an officer of the law, Emmy. I won't lie, even for you. Not only do I have a responsibility to uphold the law, I've got to answer to the Lord, too. I used to think you were the same."

Emma felt the sting of his words like a sharp slap in the face. What had happened to her? Sneaking around, lying, ruining her reputation. She had much to ask forgiveness for, starting with Nate.

"You're right Nate, I'm sorry." She walked across the room, looking up at him with remorse. "I hope you'll forgive me. It's just all this stress I've been under, that's all. It's making me act crazy."

Nate nodded, his eyes still cold. "Sure. I understand. Now, we'd better get you home before your mother has a nervous breakdown."

Home. Was someone watching her house right now, waiting for the next opportunity to strike? Fear danced a crazy jig up her spine and for a desperate moment she looked back at Tyler. Oh, to just stay here, in his arms, where no one would hurt her. What in the world was she thinking? There were people out searching for her, worried. People she had known all her life. Tyler was just a seasonal guest, someone she hardly knew. Emma's inner resolve hardened and she straightened her shoulders.

"I need to go. I'm sorry, you know, about everything."

"You don't owe me an apology, Em. We're friends, remember. You'll be okay?" Tyler asked, as if sensing her sudden fear.

"Yes, yes I will." Emma raised her chin a notch. "Whoever is doing this has destroyed enough already. I can't let them steal my peace of mind, my security, or my reputation. I won't."

"Okay." Tyler nodded once. "But remember what I said about that stubborn streak Emma, don't let it get you hurt."

Every light was ablaze in her house as Emma pulled into her driveway. The stark remains of her decimated garage shone briefly in her headlights and once again she had to fight the fear that assailed her. She *would* be alright. Lo though I walk through the valley of the shadow of death, I will fear no evil, she told herself as she got out of the car.

Nate parked his cruiser at the curb as she walked to the front door. The one that used to welcome her home, the one that had made her feel so safe and secure. So proud. The thought landed a blow to her heart. She had been proud, almost to the point of conceit, Emma admitted. One more sin in a long list she seemed to be compiling these days.

Oh Lord, help me, please, forgive me and give me strength, Emma prayed as she opened the front door and walked inside.

"Emma! Oh, Emma!" Her mother rushed to her side as she entered the living room. "Ed! It's Emma! Nate found her!"

Relief slowly replaced worry on her father's face as he came from the kitchen. "Where have you been? We've been scared to death! We thought for sure that maniac had kidnapped you!"

"I'm sorry, so sorry," Emma gave her mother a tight hug and felt the familiar, secure arms circle her. "I needed to talk to someone, that's all. I was so tired, I fell asleep. I didn't mean to frighten you, honestly I didn't."

Nate cleared his throat as Carolynn passed Emma into her father's arms.

"I've never been so scared in my life, baby."

"Oh Daddy, I didn't mean to scare you. I just, I had to get out of here and I didn't want to tell anyone. I knew you would tell me not to go. It was selfish of me, I can see that now."

"But Emma, who did you go see?" Carolynn asked. "We called Rhonda and everyone else we could think of, no one had seen you."

Emma felt Nate poke her in the shoulder, another reminder to tell the whole truth and nothing but the truth, so help her God. What were her parents going to think? It didn't matter, she reminded herself. She knew the truth. God knew the truth. She had to walk in truth. Emma took a deep breath.

"Actually, I went out to see Tyler. Nothing happened, really. No matter what some people might think." She threw an accusing look over her shoulder. "I just wanted to talk to him, that's all. I fell asleep on his couch and that's the truth."

She had failed. As Emma lay in bed her mind went over the events of the past week and her glaring mistakes stood out like giant dragons, ready to devour her. Fallen flat on her face, that's what she'd done. Every move she had made, while giving lip service to the Lord, was to further her own agenda, not God's. She had stuck her nose in where it didn't belong, been suspicious of people she had known her whole life, and practically ran into the arms of a man she hardly knew. She had given in to worry and pride, and taken up lying. Oh Lord, she was a mess!

Father, forgive me. I don't know what's happening to me. I don't know where to turn, or who to trust. I can't even trust myself anymore. I know I've let You down, I know I failed whatever test You were giving me. I just don't know why this is happening!

Trust in the Lord with all your heart, and lean not on your own understanding; in all your ways acknowledge Him, and He shall direct your paths.

It was as if someone whispered the words from Proverbs in her ear. Emma recognized the truth. She had not been relying on the Lord, she had been trying to figure things out on her own, rushing headlong into the fray, trying to solve the case herself. Where was her faith, her trust?

Lord, I know I've made a mess of things. I've lacked trust, I've questioned Your judgement, I've been a lousy witness. I'm truly sorry for how I've failed. Thank you that in my weakness, You are strong. Thank you that tomorrow is a new day, a clean slate, a chance to do better. And thank You that Your grace is sufficient for me. Amen.

Emma fell asleep, cleansed, knowing she was forgiven and determined to do better tomorrow.

CHAPTER NINETEEN

"I really am sorry about last night, Mom," Emma said as she and her mother worked in the Spot of Tea's kitchen the next morning. She looked down into the bowl of batter she was stirring, trying to gain courage. "I need to ask your forgiveness. I feel horrible that I caused you so much worry, and, I'm sorry that I, you know, compromised myself by going out to Tyler's cabin."

"Oh honey, of course I forgive you." Carolynn took Emma in her arms. "We all make mistakes, we're human, even you." She laughed and took Emma's face between her hands. "I can understand you going to Tyler. He's a very handsome man, and there's something about him that commands trust. If you were going to damage your reputation, which I know you haven't and never would, I could understand it happening with Tyler."

"Yes, well." Emma turned away, coloring slightly. She cleared her throat and went back to mixing batter. "It won't be happening again, I can assure you. I had a long talk with the Lord last night. I realized I was trying to get my safety and security through people. Through having you and Dad here, having Nate around, and Tyler. No more. Today's a new day, I'm a new woman and I'm trusting God to take care of me. I can't be running to every Tom, Dick and Harry the minute a problem arises. And Tyler, well, he'll be going back to the city eventually," Emma fought to get the words past the lump in her throat. "I can't get too used to relying on him. The Lord is big enough to protect me. Starting today, I'm making Him my all and all."

"Emma honey, of course the Lord wants to be first in your life, but He puts people in our lives for good reason. Needing people isn't weak. I don't pretend to know God's plan, but I'm not sure that you should cut Tyler out of the picture completely."

"No Mom, my mind is made up. I've seen the light. A week ago I helped Tyler find his way back to the Lord and all I've done since then is be a witness to a weak faith and questionable morals. You know that last night, I wanted to lie? I even asked Nate to lie, too. No more. The Lord doesn't want us to just give Him lip service. He wants to see fruit. That's what I'm going to do, start bearing some fruit. That's the best thing I can do for Tyler. You know he came up here with a lot of hurts and problems of his own. I'm the one that told him to give them to God, that God would see him through. I need to start practicing what I preach."

"I think you are being far too hard on yourself.

You have more faith than anyone I know. Every day you're a living witness. God put Tyler here, in this place, at this time, for His good reason. We can't be too quick to think we know what that reason is." Carolynn looked steadily at her daughter. Emma turned away, busying herself with sliding muffin tins into the large wall oven.

"I know the Lord put Tyler here for a reason. He sent him here to heal, physically and spiritually. God wanted Tyler to come back to Himself, and that's what's happened. Tyler's greatest desire is to be able to go back to work, and I know the Lord will make him able to do that. Now I have to trust that the Lord will fulfill His purpose where I'm concerned. All this vandalism and the threats. I've spent a lot of time asking 'why God?' The Lord is showing me, showing me my pride, how my confidence has come so often from myself and my accomplishments. Daddy told me this was a test, and I'm sure it is. I plan to pass that test and I don't believe I can do that by leaning on all the people around me." No matter how attractive and enticing they may be, Emma thought to herself.

Carolynn shook her head and sighed.

"It seems you have the Lord all figured out honey. Just be careful. God warns us that His ways are not our ways. Just when you think you have the world all figured out, the Lord loves to throw you a curve ball."

The silver bell above the tea shop door set to tinkling, warning Emma more customers had arrived. She turned to see Tyler walking across the threshold. Her heart did a stutter step, her breath catching in her throat. She groaned inwardly. Here he was, bigger, stronger, more handsome than the image she had held in her mind all day. Every cell in her body seemed to reach out toward him, yearned to go to him, feel his arms around her once more.

No! Absolutely not, she warned herself. She forced herself to turn away, back toward the kitchen, away from the eyes that were searching her out. It took every ounce of strength she had for Emma to purposely pick up a green order ticket and begin filling it when all she really wanted to do was run back out front and melt into Tyler's arms.

"The Lord is my strength and my shield, in Him will I put my trust. For we are more than conquerors with Christ Jesus," Emma muttered as she reached for cups and saucers from the cupboard in front of her.

"Hey you, we need to talk." Tyler's soft voice and his breath brushing against her ear sent Emma spinning, the delicate china flying from her suddenly numb fingers. "Careful there." Tyler reached for the falling cup as Emma grabbed for the saucer. Their hands became knotted but they managed to capture the pieces of delicate glass before they hit the floor. Tyler handed the cup back to her, a quizzical look on his face. "You okay, you seem a little jumpy."

"Me? No, I'm fine." Emma turned away quickly, the cup and saucer rattling as her shaking hands tried to arrange them on a tray.

Her heart raced at his nearness. Go away! She wanted to shout at him. How was she ever going to keep her promises to the Lord with Tyler literally breathing down her neck? She tried to steady her nerves as she purposely kept her back to him, peering closely at the order ticket once more. Emma reached deep, deep within herself and found a last fragment of stubborn resolve. She pulled away from him as much as space permitted and stiffened her backbone.

"You're right, we do need to talk, but right now isn't really the best time. I'm awfully busy." From somewhere Emma found the strength to turn around. She lightly put fingertips to Tyler's chest and pushed him a step away from her.

Tilting his head, Tyler scratched the bridge of his nose with a forefinger.

"There's only a few people in the dining room, I'm sure your mom and the other girl can handle it."

"It's not their business to handle, it's mine." Emma stepped around Tyler's broad form and went to the stove where she purposefully picked up a tea kettle. "This is the busiest time of the year and…"

"Emma." The warning tone in Tyler's voice made Emma turn around. He was staring at her, hands on hips. The look in his eyes told her he would put up with none of her nonsense. She sighed. Okay, she had to change tactics.

"Alright, let me just tell Mom we are stepping out for a minute, then we'll talk."

Tyler watched Emma carefully as she perched on the edge of the picnic table. She smoothed the fabric of her red sun dress over her knees repeatedly. He tried not to dwell on the way the clingy knit fabric hugged her curves. The red, white and blue ribbons that held Emma's ponytail whipped in the breeze. She turned her face into the wind, away from Tyler's steady gaze and reached up to secure them more tightly. Once more his eyes were drawn to her curves. He forced himself to look away.

"So," they both began at the same time then laughed nervously. Emma finally looked Tyler full in the face, folding her hands in her lap.

"What is it you think we need to talk about, Em?" Tyler was all serious business now.

"I need to ask your forgiveness."

"My forgiveness? What for?"

"For my behavior last night, for starters." Emma looked down at the hands in her lap. "My behavior since you arrived here, really, but last night in particular."

"You didn't do anything to be forgiven for."

"Oh yes, yes, I did." Emma nodded as a sad smile tilted up one corner of her lips. She continued to stare at her hands. "I'm afraid I've been giving you mixed signals since you came to town. One minute throwing myself at your feet, the next minute insisting we be friends. You told me where you stand and I respect that. Last night, coming to you, it was wrong. Can you forgive me?"

"Listen, Em, I don't see what I should forgive you for. It's not like you came to me for, for nefarious purposes." Oh but what if she had? Tyler pushed away the thought and continued. "We both know last night was completely innocent, no matter what Nate

Sweeney might elude to. You needed someone to talk to, and you picked me. I feel honored, which leads me to what I feel we really need to talk about." Tyler took a deep breath and asked, "Who is Adam?"

He watched closely as Emma's hands stopped toying with her dress.

"Who are you talking about?" she asked quietly. "I never mentioned anyone named Adam."

"Oh yes, you did sweetheart." Tyler leaned closer, his eyes boring into hers. "As you were falling asleep, the name just sort of slipped from your lips." His eyes fell to her beautiful, bow shaped mouth. He resisted the urge to kiss her lie away. "I want to know who he is and what you know. I want you to tell me the truth." His voice was low, a near whisper fluttering over Emma's skin, persuading her.

Emma jumped up from the picnic table.

"It doesn't matter. I told you last night, I don't really know anything. I was wrong to come to you for help and involve you in my problems." Emma backed away from him, toward the kitchen door of the shop. "You have your own troubles and the Lord is showing me that I need to rely on Him, not people. I just hope you can forgive me. I promise, I won't bother you any more." Emma reached the kitchen door, quickly yanked it open and disappeared inside.

Tyler leaned an elbow on the picnic table and put his head in his hand. What were they doing to each other? Playing their game of cat and mouse, of let's pretend we're just friends. He almost laughed at Emma's empty promise to not bother him anymore. If she only knew what the mere thought of her did to his heart. Bothered him aplenty. Who was he fooling? Emma wasn't the only one giving mixed signals, he was just as guilty. One minute insisting he was leaving at the end of the summer, the next trying to play her hero.

The door where Emma had disappeared stood like a barrier between them. He hadn't gotten the answers to any of his questions, not about Adam or about their relationship. Tyler slapped his jean clad thighs and stood. He looked around the town with narrowed eyes. He wanted to go but he wanted to stay. What did the Lord want him to do? He had time to figure it out, and in the mean time he had made a promise to Emma's mother, and he planned to make good on it. Emma need never know that someone else was helping the Lord look out for her welfare.

Emma walked straight from the kitchen out into the small dining room, pushing Tyler from her mind and focusing instead on business. She looked around at the few tables that were occupied which Rhonda was easily handling. Her mother sat at the corner table, sipping a cup of tea. Emma sat down across from her.

"So, did you and Tyler have a nice little talk?" Carolynn asked.

She didn't want to tell another lie. Emma searched for the right words.

"I think Tyler and I have come to an understanding."

Emma felt the sharp stab of pain go directly through her heart. The scene out back had probably been their final goodbye. She had promised Tyler she wouldn't bother him anymore and she intended to keep that promise. It was better this way. Putting herself in his path constantly would only prolong the pain when he left at the end of the summer.

"What kind of understanding is that?" Carolynn couldn't mask her curiosity.

Emma let out a long breath, blowing strands of dark hair from her eyes.

"That the way I've been behaving was wrong and that I need to stop using him as a crutch. Tyler needs to concentrate on himself from now on. That's all."

"Oh, Emma. Are you sure this is what you want?"

"I'm trying to learn that it's not all about what I want, Mom." Emma toyed with the cloth on the table, folding and refolding tiny pleats in the linen. "If it was up to me, I'd beg Tyler to stay here forever. I, I'm pretty sure I've gone and fallen in love with him." There, she'd said it. The whole truth and nothing but the truth. She saw the empathy pouring from her mother's eyes. "Tyler can't know. It would ruin everything. His main focus has to be on returning to his job. That's what he needs more than anything, and I have to leave him alone so he can achieve it."

"That all sounds very noble, but…"

"I'm not trying to be noble," Emma cut off her mother's objections. "I'm trying to do what I honestly feel is best. Tyler has his own life and I have mine. So, what do you say we have a picnic at the park tonight? A band is playing in the pavilion this evening and Dad can fish if he wants. It would be fun, don't you think?" She forced enthusiasm she didn't feel.

"There will be lots of people there and you guys can catch up with all your old friends. I had wanted to have a barbecue, but well, there's no way I could sit out on my patio and look at that garage." The image of her burned out carriage house rose into Emma's mind, momentarily blocking out all other thoughts. She pushed away the despondency that tried to settle over her and forced a cheerful smile. "This will be better anyway, more exciting with all the people around and some good music. I think they're playing bluegrass. Come on, say yes." She squeezed her mother's hand where it lay on the table.

"Okay dear, let's do it. Some fun will do us all good."

* * *

Tyler casually walked through downtown Atlanta, examining everything and everyone he saw. There was no doubt in his mind that whoever was threatening Emma was just waiting for the next opportunity to strike. How could he prevent it without her knowing what he was up to?

He could go to Sweeney and tell him the name. Tyler dismissed the thought as quickly as it had come. Sweeney would most likely laugh and accuse him of conjuring up a name just to get himself off the hook. And Emma would never confess to knowing anything. That was a fact Tyler knew he could bet his life on. As pretty and soft and sweet as she appeared, she sure was made of sterner, more stubborn stuff on the inside. Tyler shook his head, admiration warring with aggravation inside him.

"Hello, Tyler!" Ed Dawson stepped from the hardware store and yelled a greeting. "What brings you to town today?" Ed asked as he fell into step beside Tyler.

"Oh, just thought I'd check things out. Looks like the town is ready for the big holiday." Tyler eyed the people who crowded the sidewalk. He had been over every inch of the town and still had no conceivable plan for protecting Emma.

"Yep, it's a big deal around here. Most excitement the town will see all year." The two men made their way toward the front door of Emma's shop. "Why don't you come in and have a cup of coffee with me?" Ed invited. "Tell me more about what you've done with the cabin."

"No, Mr. Dawson, really, I shouldn't." Tyler hesitated at the door. "I've got things I need to do." Tyler's heart pounded as the old man urged him closer to the door.

"Don't be ridiculous, Tyler. That's the great thing about up here. You never have to hurry. You've got the whole summer, right?" Ed held the door open, looking up at Tyler expectantly.

"Yeah, right, the whole summer." Tyler stepped across the threshold, knowing it was a mistake. Every moment spent in Emma's presence was another moment ticked off the clock, bringing him closer to the time he would have to leave her. A reality that got harder to swallow with each passing day.

"Edward, I need you to go to the store and get some things for tonight." Carolynn stepped to the table as Ed sat down. She draped a loving arm over his shoulder and exchanged a knowing look with Tyler. "Emma's suggested we have a picnic at the park this evening. There's going to be a band and everything. Doesn't that sound like fun? You're welcome to come too, Tyler, if you would like."

Tyler recognized the opportunity as it was falling into his lap. He read the unspoken message in Carolynn's eyes, reminding him of the promise he had made. This was his chance to see if he could make good on his word. But joining the family, that was out of the question. He had to keep his distance. Each moment spent in Emma's presence just added to the agony of leaving her eventually. No more mixed signals.

"I'm sorry, Mrs. Dawson, I would love to join you, but I have something else I have to do tonight."

CHAPTER TWENTY

T he sky still held a portion of the day's bright-
ness when Emma and her parents found an
empty picnic table at the township park. Emma
shook out a checked table cloth, watching as it
billowed out then settled over the rough wood.
Would Adam be here, watching her? The thought
made her skin crawl. But if Adam was here, then he
wouldn't be getting into mischief somewhere else.

For all her earlier bravado, Emma had balked at
leaving her house unattended. What if it was the next
thing to be set on fire? She and her parents had said a
prayer, right there on her front porch, asking God to
set a guard over her house, and if not, then His will
be done. The act had set Emma's mind at ease, but
now here in the park, with people milling all around,
she once again felt anxious and vulnerable.

"Edward, over here!" Carolynn called and
waved an arm over her head as Ed came trudging
toward them carrying a cooler.

Emma watched as her father put the cooler down at one end of the table and dropped a quick kiss on Carolynn's mouth. The two exchanged a loving glance that put a hook in Emma's heart. As if they had a mind of their own, her eyes scanned the crowded park, searching for any sign of Tyler. Emma caught herself in the act and gave herself a shake. She had heard her mother issue the invitation to join them, and she had heard Tyler decline. She should have been relieved, so why did her traitorous heart insist on being disappointed. Didn't it realize Tyler had better things to do?

The evening held little appeal for Emma, but she put on her brave face and smiled though she felt like crying. Every flash of the setting sun on a blond head made her turn, hoping to see Tyler. Every teenage boy with dark hair had her skin going goosebumpy with fear. The emotional roller coaster drained Emma of all energy. Cast your cares upon the Lord, she kept telling herself. Why was that so hard to do?

When the trio of musicians took their place on the raised platform of the pavilion, Emma concentrated on the music, trying to lose her thoughts in the melody with no success. She continued to glance around, her heart longing for Tyler. Emma looked wistfully at her parents. They stood side by side, sometimes with their arms around one another, sometimes clapping along with the music. Their eyes shone with enjoyment and Emma couldn't help but smile as Ed looked down and gave his wife a quick kiss.

Everyone made such a fuss about young love, ah, but to have old love, aged to perfection, that seemed so much better to Emma. Would she ever find the same? As if it had never left, the image of Tyler planted itself firmly in Emma's mind. This time she didn't force it away, instead she allowed herself to imagine, if only for a moment, then sent up a silent prayer.

At the edge of the parking lot, dark blue baseball cap pulled low over his eyes, stood Tyler, his keen gaze never leaving Emma. For the past few hours he had watched jealously as she laughed and talked with her family and the many townspeople who stopped to talk with them. Now she was standing with the others, listening to the music, her dark ponytail swaying provocatively as she moved with the rhythm. It was torture to stay so far away from her, but Tyler knew it was best. From his vantage point he could see every person who moved toward her and though he appeared to be lounging against the car behind him, his body was coiled, ready to spring into action should the need arise.

Anxiety stole over him like a dark shadow. Would he really be able to respond quickly enough if a crisis arose? Since the accident, Tyler hadn't been able to even think of climbing back into a rescue squad. For the past couple of months he had doubted if he would ever be able to resume the job he had loved. Deep down he worried that he had lost the instincts it took to save lives. If Emma's life hung in the balance, could he pull through for her? He honestly didn't know. But Tyler did know that already his brief stay here in the north woods had begun to heal him, had restored him at least partially to himself. He had to hope, and believe, that if Emma was in danger, the Lord would make him able to respond.

"Hey buddy, this your car?"

Tyler froze at the sound of Nate Sweeney's voice. Slowly he straightened away from the hood of the car on which he had been leaning.

"Actually, no Officer, it isn't." Slowly Tyler turned to face the deputy. Nate's eyes went hard and glittered like shards of ice.

"So, it's Mr. McGillis." Nate leaned back and crossed his arms. "What brings you into town, looking to stir up a little more trouble?"

"That implies that you think I've stirred up trouble before, Deputy." Tyler, too, crossed his arms, facing the officer four square. The two men faced off for several seconds, toe to toe, the bill of Tyler's ball cap nearly touching the brim of Nate's hat. "I'm just a visitor around here." Tyler shrugged one broad shoulder and turned back to see where Emma was. "I came to watch some of the festivities, and keep any eye on things, if you know what I mean."

Frantically his eyes searched the crowd around the pavilion, looking for Emma's dark head and red dress. His heart momentarily stopped beating when he saw she was no longer with her parents. Relief washed over him when he finally spied her talking to Rhonda.

"You've caused more trouble than you think,

McGillis. I'm warning you, watch your step around Emma. She's thought of real highly around here and there's plenty of us who don't take kindly to you playing your big city games with her. You're going to go back where you came from and if you aren't real careful you'll leave Emma with a bad reputation and a whole lot of hurt. If those were punishable offenses, I'd gladly lock you up in a heartbeat."

Tyler heard the jealously behind the officer's words and almost smirked. He had to bite his tongue from saying 'too bad, but she doesn't love you, buddy,' but he managed to suppress the urge. Instead he took the high ground, giving a mock salute as he walked away.

"Point taken, Deputy Sweeney. Rest assured that I'll try real hard to make sure Emma doesn't get hurt." Not in any way, he added to himself.

Tyler walked toward the crowd, trying to get a better view of Emma. He froze as she walked away from the people assembled around the musicians and made her way alone toward the parking lot. What was she doing, trying to make herself a sitting duck for trouble? Two teenage boys approached her and Tyler slipped behind a tree, poised to intervene should the two make any threatening moves. He breathed a sigh of relief as he heard Emma say,

"Hey Kirt, hey Jesse, what are you guys up to tonight?"

"Well Miz Dawson, Kirt is trying to get Brandy Corbin's attention and you should see…"

"Shut up twerp!" The taller boy slugged the younger one in the shoulder.

"It's true!"

"It is not!"

"I think Brandy is a lovely girl," Emma said diplomatically. "You have very good taste, Kirt. I think I saw her right down there, by the river. If I remember correctly, she was with Chelsea. Isn't Chelsea about your age, Jesse?"

"Ooh, ick. I'm not into that stuff, Miz Dawson. Girls are yucky, well, except you, of course."

"Well, thank you." Emma laughed and pleasure skimmed across Tyler's heart at the sound. "You have plenty of time for all that girl stuff. So, why don't you let Kirt go say hi to Brandy and you can walk me up to my dad's car to get my sweater. I'm not supposed to go anywhere alone you know."

"Cool! Thanks Miss Dawson." The older boy pushed his friend's shoulder before heading briskly down the hill toward the river.

"Why aren't you supposed to be going anywhere alone?" Tyler followed from a distance as Emma and the other boy walked to the parking lot. He ducked behind a pick up as Emma unlocked the door of her father's car. "Is it cuz of what happened with your garage burning down?"

"I'm afraid so, Jesse." There was an unmistakable sadness in Emma's voice. "Remember when I told you and Kirt about the roses, that there was a note? Well, this time there was a note, too. This makes three times now someone has threatened me. Four if you count the graffiti on my fence."

"Wow," Jesse's voice held a touch of awe. He looked around the parking lot, bravery and fear battling in his teenage body. "So the cops think someone wants to hurt you for real?"

"It appears that could be the case. Have you and Kirt heard anything, you know, any of the kids talking?" Emma's voice started to fade and Tyler realized the two were walking back toward the park. He quickly followed, trying to keep his distance yet straining to hear their conversation.

"Naw, we haven't heard nothin'. But with school out, we don't see that many kids anymore. You still thinkin' Adam mighta done it?"

Ah, Tyler smiled to himself. So, Emma wouldn't confide in him, but she trusted these two teenagers enough to let them in on her suspicions. He filed that information away for later use. Emma stopped to put her arms through the sleeves of her sweater, turning slightly to face Jesse. Tyler stepped behind a small group of trees, trying to hold his breath so he could hear Emma's answer.

"I don't know Jesse, I really don't. Probably not. I mean, why would he?"

"I told ya Miz Dawson, he's weird."

"Jesse, that's not nice. You know Adam's had it rough. What he really needs is friends, people to care about him."

The boy practically snorted. "Trust me Miz Dawson, he don't want no friends. If he does, he has a very weird way of showing it."

"Well, I don't really even know him, so what could he possibly have against me to want to hurt me? I can't think of a thing, which means it was probably just nerves making me see things that weren't there."

"Me and Kirt, we'll still keep an eye out. We'll let you know if we hear anything."

"Thanks Jesse, you'd better go on, I think I see Kirt coming this way and it looks like Brandy and Chelsea are with him. Have fun."

"Oh, ick," Jesse grumbled as he headed toward the three teenagers coming up the hill.

Tyler's intense green eyes followed Emma as she walked back toward the pavilion. The skirt of her dress swayed invitingly, creating a hollow longing within him. The attraction he had felt since first meeting Emma had quickly grown beyond his control and Tyler knew he was no longer able to fight it. It was taking a big risk, falling for Emma Dawson. She could cut him open just as brutally as that windshield glass had done three months ago. Did he really want to add another scar to the others that would mar him for the rest of his life?

He saw Emma approach her parents, saw them open their arms and welcome her back into their circle. Tyler knew with crystal clarity that he really was healed from the past because he was willing to risk his life again, no doubt about it.

CHAPTER TWENTY ONE

Though the Fourth of July would go out with the loud bangs of fireworks, it came in with a quiet whisper, the wind sighing gently as dawn nudged the sky. As Emma unlocked the front door to the Spot of Tea, she looked up at the velvety darkness. The stars slowly winked out one by one. What would the day bring? She had always loved this holiday, the patriotic fervor, the fun, the camaraderie of being an American.

This year she just wanted it over and done. After two tense days, Emma wasn't sure she was up to the crowds, the noise, the pressure. She really just wanted to go somewhere quiet where she could curl up and sleep for a month of Sundays. Emma squared her shoulders. She had a business to run. The Lord would give her the strength to get through one more day.

Carolynn was beside her as she pulled open the plate glass door to the shop. Out of habit Emma stepped into the darkened dining room and headed straight toward the kitchen. She immediately tripped and fell.

"Ow! What in the world?" Emma lay on the floor in the dark. Sharp, stinging pain bit into her arms and legs.

"Emma, are you okay?" Carolynn asked. "What is it?" She reached behind her to the switches by the door. Bright light bathed the dining room, exposing the disaster around them.

"Ohhh noooo," Emma cried in stunned disbelief. "No, no, no." Hot tears of dismay burned her eyes as she looked around the restaurant. Tables and chairs were upended, table cloths strewn about the floor. A trail of broken glass led back to the kitchen. Carefully Emma picked herself up from the floor, brushing shards of crushed china from her arms. Slowly she righted the chair she had tripped over.

"We've got to get out of here." Carolynn grabbed Emma's arm and yanked her back out the door.

"Mother!" Emma began to protest.

"He could be in there, Emma, waiting in the kitchen."

Waves of terror washed over Emma, making her shiver in the cool, pre-dawn air. She put her face in her hands. This couldn't be happening, it was all a nightmare, just a bad dream.

"We've got to call Nate, come on honey." Carolynn tried to move Emma toward the car. Emma dropped her hands as fury, hot as the fires of Hades began to burn within her.

"So we go in the kitchen and call him." Emma moved toward the back door of the shop. "I hope to high heaven that whoever did this is in there, because if he is, I swear I'm going to beat the living daylights out of him!"

"No, honey, don't go in there!" Carolynn tried to catch Emma as she stomped toward the door. "It's dangerous, you don't know what this person is capable of!" Carolynn grabbed at her daughter. Emma ignored her mother's desperate plea.

"Yeah, and they don't know what I'm capable of either." With trembling hands Emma fumbled with the key to the back door only to find she didn't need it. The lock had been jimmied and the door stood slightly ajar. Emma pushed it open with far more force than was necessary. The door banged loudly against the wall, sounding like a shot in the still room.

"Anybody in here?" she yelled. "I hope you are you no good, slimy, poor excuse for a human being!"

Fiercely Emma jerked up the light switch by the door. With the light came the revelation of more destruction throughout the kitchen. She wanted to swear, wanted to scream, wanted to punch somebody's lights out. Except for the mess, the kitchen was empty. Cupboards stood open, their contents hurled around the room. The refrigerator yawned open, food dumped everywhere on the floor. She picked her way through broken glass, flour, tea bags and chicken salad to the phone on the wall. Numb fingers punched in the number to the sheriff's department.

"Someone might be hiding in the bathrooms," Carolynn whispered from the door, unable to force herself across the threshold.

"I hope to God they are," Emma said through clenched teeth. She yanked open drawers, searching, finally spied what she was looking for under a mass of now soiled dishtowels. She picked up the large knife, clutching it in a white knuckled hand. "I hope to God they are."

An eternity seemed to pass before Emma saw the flashing lights of a police cruiser through the still open back door, but in reality it was mere minutes. She stood in her destroyed kitchen, the knife held in a death grip. Everything was a blur as officers swarmed over the building. Her father arrived, her mother was crying. It was Nate who finally pried the knife from her hand.

"You're bleeding." He turned Emma's delicate hand over in his own, exposing the cuts down the outside of her palm.

"It must have happened when I fell," Emma said in a wooden voice, taking no notice of the blood. Suddenly she grabbed Nate by his shirt front, staining his meticulous uniform. Her hot eyes bored into him. "Nate, you have got to catch this guy, you have to. I want him dead, I want him beaten to a pulp, you've got to make this stop!" The tears she had been holding back burst through the dam of her bravado, crumpling her with massive sobs.

"Shhhh, Emmy, we will, I promise." He wrapped his arms around her. "We're going to catch this guy, everything is going to be okay."

"And you'll shoot him? Better yet, let me shoot him." Tears coursed down her red cheeks as she looked imploringly up at Nate.

"You don't really mean that Emma," Nate said softly. "You don't really want that kind of justice."

"Yes I do!" Emma angrily pushed away from him. Tortured eyes looked around, seeing her dream destroyed. She dropped her face into her hands, shoulders still shaking with sobs. She tried to swallow the hysteria that was close to overcoming her. Finally she lifted her head, swiped a hand under her nose and said tiredly, "Just catch him Nate, okay, just catch him."

The Spot of Tea would do no business that day. Emma tried not to think of the money she was losing. The Lord would provide. They couldn't even start on clean up. The shop was a crime scene, roped off with yellow police tape. The investigators would have to go over every inch of the place, looking for fingerprints and other evidence.

The July sun had risen hot and brilliant in the cloudless sky by the time Emma and her parents drove the short distance from the shop to her home. She grimaced as they pulled into the driveway. The charred remains of her garage stood as a reminder that there was no escape from the destruction that closed in around her.

Anger, cold and merciless filled her heart, shocking Emma with her new-found capacity for hatred. Just hours ago she had declared she wanted her tormentor dead. It scared her, how true that was. Being refined in the fire was sure a hard business. She didn't like some of the elements of her character that were being revealed.

Tiredly she got out of the car and followed her parents to the door. The urge to turn tail and run was strong. For the first time, the idea of selling out settled in her mind. She could go downstate to live with her parents, far from the clutches of whoever was determined to ruin her. And closer to Tyler, the unbidden thought danced across her brain. Emma quickly pushed it aside. It had nothing to do with Tyler and everything to do with being safe. She just wanted to be safe! Everything within her rebelled at the thought of leaving, selling her house, abandoning her business. Her whole life was here, in this town. She couldn't imagine herself anywhere else.

As she climbed the stairs to her room, Emma knew without a doubt that she had only one choice. She had to stay and see this thing through to the end, whatever that entailed. The Lord would see her through, wouldn't He? Emma paused on the stairs, her faith wavering. Where had God been last night when the vandal broke into her shop? Where had He been when her garage was set on fire? Was He even listening to her paltry prayers?

Lo, I am with you always, even to the end of the age.

Yes, Emma had to believe He was here, right beside her, right now, through all of this. There was no alternative. As she proceeded up the stairs, Emma knew she had to reach beyond her own hurt and trust the Lord.

Tyler couldn't believe the sight that met his eyes

as he pulled into the parking lot of Emma's shop. Two county police cruisers and a blue state trooper vehicle sat in front of the restaurant. Yellow tape made a barrier around the building. Heart pounding, Tyler jumped from his truck, his thoughts only on Emma and the fact that something must have happened to her. Without hesitation he ducked under the tape and headed for the door. A burly deputy blocked his path.

"Hey buddy, this is a crime scene. Off limits. You can't go in there."

"Where's Emma, is she okay?" Tyler tried to shake off the hand that held his arm. "I just want to know if something's happened to her!"

"She's not in the building." The deputy stood his ground, stepping sideways when Tyler made a move to go around him.

"Then where is she, is she okay?" Tyler fought to rein in his run away emotions as he stepped back from the door and ran a shaky hand over his face. Inspiration hit him. "Is Sweeney here?"

The deputy shot him a questioning look, hesitating several seconds before nodding.

"Yeah, he's in there. Hey Nate!" the deputy called over his shoulder into the open kitchen door.

"What is it?" Nate rushed to the door, alarmed.

"Someone here asking for you." The deputy hooked a thumb at Tyler then disappeared inside.

Nate came to a halt, relief and dislike washing over his features.

"What do you want, McGillis?"

"What happened?" Tyler nodded toward the door.

Nate crossed his arms, looking at Tyler through narrowed eyes.

"Why do you want to know?"

"Look, is Emma alright? That's all I care about."

Nate uncrossed his arms, looking over his shoulder before stepping down onto the back stoop.

"Emma's fine, physically. She went home a little while ago. Someone broke in here last night and did a lot of damage. It's a mess." He shook his dark head and looked Tyler straight in the eye. Tyler saw the internal battle Nate was fighting. The deputy seemed to come to a decision. He took a deep breath.

"As much as it pains me to admit this to you of all people, I'm worried. I've got a parade to keep in order this afternoon, drunks to keep off the street, kids with fireworks to keep from blowing themselves up. Our department is short staffed as it is, and now we've got this. I don't doubt for a minute that someone is going to try and hurt Emma, my doubt is whether or not we can keep it from happening."

"Why are you telling me this?"

"Because I know there's something going on between you two, and as much as I don't like it, I have to face the facts. And the fact is, I can't be by Emma's side all day today, as much as I would like that responsibility. And I would like it." Nate's eyes conveyed his meaning.

"I have a job to do. Her parents, bless their hearts, aren't exactly hero material. Someone is going to have to keep on eye on that girl, someone who can actually do something if someone tries to hurt her. That's what you were doing at the park last night, if I'm not mistaken. Mrs. Dawson might not think I'm the smartest cop who ever walked the beat, but I'm privy to a lot more than she gives me credit for. I'm giving you a heads up. Whoever's been doing this stuff is serious, and dangerous. I'm going to trust you'll keep Emma out of harm's way."

Keep Emma out of harm's way. How was he going to do that? Tyler wondered as he drove the short distance to Emma's house. Stick to her like glue, he decided. No more skulking around behind trees, no matter how much she might protest having a bodyguard. She had to realize by now that she needed protection, human as well as divine.

His palms were sweating. Tyler wiped them on the sides of his jeans as Carolynn knocked on Emma's bedroom door.

"Emma, honey, you have a visitor." Carolynn turned the knob and pushed the door open slightly.

"Tell them to go away," Emma grumbled. She turned her face toward the door, eyes going wide at the sight of Tyler. Scrambling, she sat upright on the bed. "You definitely go away," she tried to sound peeved.

"I'm wounded." Tyler put a hand over his heart. His mouth tipped up in a half smile as he walked into the room with more confidence than he actually felt.

Emma reminded him of himself, just a few short months ago. How many times had he told friends and family, doctors and nurses to go away and leave him alone? Too many. They had only been trying to help and he had stubbornly refused. He needed to make

Emma see what he had been blind to back then.

Tyler sauntered toward the bed, looking around the feminine room with its pale pink wallpaper and white lace curtains. It was the perfect reflection of the woman in front of him; soft, innocent, pure. He nudged her legs over so he could sit on the edge of the bed, trying to ignore the view of shapely calves and small feet. He noticed her toenails were painted bright red. Always a surprise, his Emma.

She sat up straighter, pulling her knees up to her chin, avoiding contact with him.

"What are you doing here?" she asked, refusing to look him in the eye.

"I came by to see how you're doing." Tyler grimaced at the words. He had hated people asking him that question after the accident. "I'm sorry. I'm not going to ask you how you're doing, because I have a pretty good idea how you're feeling right now."

"How could you know anything about it? My life has been ripped out from under me. My business is in shambles, my property destroyed. Everything I've believed to be true, gone up in smoke. I don't even know myself anymore." Tears spilled over and Emma covered her face with her hands. "I just want to be left alone Tyler. Just leave me alone."

"I do know how you feel." Tyler's fingers encircled her delicate wrist, pulling her hand away from her face. "Because that's exactly how I felt after this happened." He traced the scar down his cheek. "I retreated. I questioned everything about myself and my life. I pushed people away for months, isolating myself, thinking that's what I needed to heal. But you know what? I was wrong.

"Even when I came up here, that's what I thought I was going to do, isolate myself in the woods until I got better. It wasn't until you came barging into my life, refusing to take no for an answer, that I started to become whole again. You know why? Because my eyes weren't on myself any more. I wasn't dwelling on my own pain. You helped me get my focus back on the Lord. And hey, when I started getting wrapped up in all your problems, mine didn't seem so bad anymore." Tyler chuckled as Emma slapped his arm.

"You are awful!" she admonished, but she was smiling as she said it. "Is that supposed to make me feel better? God sent disaster on me so you could get your act together?"

"No." Tyler shook his head. Serious again, he took Emma's hand in his, examining each fine boned finger, measuring her tiny ones against his own. It pleased him that she didn't pull away from his grip. He turned her hand palm up and saw the series of cuts down the side of her hand and wrist.

"What's this?"

Emma tried to pull her hand away but he held it, gently but firmly.

"It's nothing, just a few cuts. When I went in the shop this morning, I fell. There was broken glass everywhere. It's no big deal."

A muscle jumped in Tyler's jaw. He ran his thumb over the cuts, thinking of what he could easily do to the guy that caused them. He swallowed his fury, concentrating instead on the opportunity for good that was being held out to them. He had to hope that Emma would see it, too. Finally he summoned the nerve to look into her eyes, the eyes that had mesmerized him from the beginning when they held such understanding and acceptance.

"I don't pretend to know God's ways, Em. I spent a long time running from Him, denying His influence on my life, even hating Him for what happened. So who am I to think I've got Him all figured out now? But, if I remember correctly, it was you who told me God has a purpose for everything that happens. That means He put us together for some reason. Think maybe we should investigate what that might be?"

Emma rested her chin on her knees. A dimple peeked out as she smiled up at him. "Maybe a little investigation wouldn't hurt. But." Her smile dimmed and the dimple disappeared. "You're going away at the end of the summer."

Tyler shrugged. "That was the original plan, but who can say what the future holds?"

Emma tugged her hand from his and rose slowly from the bed. Tyler watched warily as she moved to the window. Lifting the curtain aside, she looked out.

"I've thought about selling, moving downstate with my parents."

"Is that what you really want?" Tyler asked, stunned.

"I don't know," the words were almost a whisper. "I don't seem to know anything anymore. I fluctuate between fear and faith practically every second. And then there's this rage. Have you ever hated someone,

I mean really hated someone?" Emma dropped the curtain and turned to face him.

"Sure, haven't we all?" Tyler knew the fury she was describing, had felt it himself just now as he looked at her battered hand.

"Not me. Not like this. This morning, when I walked into my shop and saw what he had done, it was like some monster came alive inside me. I picked up a knife and I honestly think, if he had been standing in front of me, I could have used it. I've never felt anything like that before in my life. It scared me."

Tyler got up from the bed and made his way over to the window. He looked out onto the remnants of her burned garage and felt once more the hot coals of anger inside him.

"I've felt hatred for this guy, too, Emma," he admitted. "You know what it reminds me of? The way I hated myself after the accident. I couldn't even look at myself in the mirror. My reflection made me physically sick. I didn't know how I would ever be able to live with that person. But instead of hurting myself or anyone else, I turned it all inward. I ate myself up with self-pity and self-loathing. Like I said before, it didn't do any good. We're all human Em, we all have human emotions. It's what we do with them that matters. God gave us free will and we have choices as to how we'll respond in different situations. I made the wrong choices after the accident. It's up to you what kind you make now."

Tyler turned away from the window. He put a finger under Emma's chin, lifting her eyes to meet his.

"I don't think you want to leave Atlanta. This is

where you belong. You've got a beautiful house and a great business. It's just my opinion, but I think you need to step out in faith and fight to keep what's yours. If you're going to sell out and move, it has to be for the right reasons, not because you're running scared."

"You're right. I already knew it, but I guess I needed to hear it from someone else." For a moment her eyes strayed once more to the window. "You know, Jesus said to bless those who curse us, do good to those who hurt us. That's an easy sermon to preach, but not so easy to put into practice. Something else I need to work on, huh?" Some of the old sparkle was back in her eyes when she turned once more to Tyler, smiling softly.

"So, what's on for today?" He forced himself to move away from her and walk across the room. He pretended to look at the photos displayed across the top of her dresser. The urge to take her in his arms and kiss her until she forgot about any outside danger nearly overwhelmed him. He needed to get his mind on something else. "I hear there's a parade and stuff going on. You up for that?"

He turned in time to see her freeze in sudden fear.

"Oh, I don't know, I don't think that's a good idea." Her dark hair swirled around her face as she shook her head. "I mean, I don't think Nate would want me wandering around town and…"

Instantly Tyler was before her. He gripped her shoulders and looked earnestly down into her frightened eyes.

"You can't stay holed up in your house forever,

Emma. Believe it or not, you're probably much safer out in public, in a crowd of people, than you are here, sitting alone." An idea struck him and his voice took on a challenging edge. "Are you going to let this guy run your life? Are you going to just throw in the towel and refuse to have fun because of what he's done? If that's the case, then you're allowing him to win. If you change your whole life because of his actions, you've given him far more power than he deserves. Is that what you want?"

Tyler was immensely satisfied to see his goading did its intended job. Emma's chin came up, determination hardening her jaw.

"Once again, you're right." Emma let out a breath, blowing her bangs from her eyes. "Good grief I'd better quit saying that or your ego is going to end up as big as Mount Everest. I highly doubt it's a good way to start off any kind of relationship, letting you think you're right all the time." She glanced over at the clock on her bedside table. The stubborn gleam was back in her eye when she looked at Tyler. "The parade starts in an hour. Just let me freshen up and we'll go."

CHAPTER TWENTY TWO

Twenty minutes later Emma descended the stairs, trembling with both anticipation and trepidation. She had changed into navy shorts and a red tank top, subduing her dark hair in a French braid. As she had gotten ready, Emma had made a decision. She wouldn't dwell on the past and she wouldn't think about the future, she would just enjoy today. That was all they were promised anyway, wasn't it?

Her parents were in the living room with Tyler, sitting amicably on the sofa, talking as if they had known each other all their lives. Emma put on a brave smile as she stepped around the banister.

"I guess we're going to go watch the parade, you guys want to come?"

"I was just telling Tyler I think that's a great idea." Ed came over and put an arm around her shoulders.

"What about the house?" Carolynn questioned,

unable to keep the concern from her voice. Emma merely shrugged.

"Well, prayer worked last night, we'll just have to rely on the same today. Plus, it's the middle of the day and there's hundreds of people in town. I doubt anyone will try anything, and if they did they would be sure to get caught. Ready?" She looked directly at Tyler. He slapped his thighs and rose from the sofa.

"Sweetheart, I was born ready." He gave her a broad wink which sent a delicious shiver over her skin while a rosy glow stained her cheeks.

"To see a parade?" she asked cheekily. "I hope you won't be disappointed. This is small town Fourth of July we're talking about here. Although we do have our own brand of patriotism here in Atlanta, it's not exactly big city excitement." Emma's breath caught as Tyler came to stand over her in the small foyer, his close proximity causing her heart to miss several beats.

"I hardly think I could be disappointed in anything Atlanta has to offer. To be honest, I've never found anything in the city that excites me quite as much as what's right here."

"Yes, well." Emma lowered her lashes, finding he was much better suited to flirtatious repartee than she. Flustered she reached for the front door and stepped out on the porch, away from his overwhelming presence. "Let's go see the parade then."

The four of them walked the short distance into town then purposely headed west, away from the Spot of Tea. The street was lined with hundreds of people, young and old alike, waving small American flags. Excitement hung heavy in the air. Tyler stayed close to Emma as she shouldered her way through the throng, looking for a good spot to view the parade. In front of the hardware store they ran into Jim and Kay Deland.

"Oh Emma, dear, we heard the horrible news." Kay squeezed Emma's upper arm and gave her a compassionate look. "How awful for you! We couldn't believe it. This whole thing seems like a terrible nightmare."

"Yup, a real bad dream for the whole town," Jim added, looking suspiciously at Tyler. "Never seen anything like it around here before."

Emma didn't care for the implication in Jim's words, but for once held her tongue.

"I'm sure Nate Sweeney will have the case solved in no time," she reassured.

"Well, you watch out for yourself now. It would break our hearts to have anything happen to you," Kay said.

"You don't have to worry." Tyler placed his warm hand on the back of Emma's neck. Small tremors of sensation danced across her skin as his thumb caressed the delicate skin just below her ear. "Emma is in good hands."

He was right about that, Emma thought, as Tyler's touch continued to wreak havoc with her insides.

"We'd better go get a spot to watch the parade before they're all taken," Emma said, stepping away from the Delands.

They headed toward the edge of town, Emma painfully, pleasantly aware of Tyler's hand that had slid from her neck to rest comfortably between her shoulder blades. How awesome it felt, this unspoken connection with another person. Emma had never experienced it before and she was struck with wonder.

As if scales had fallen from her eyes, Emma was suddenly blinded by the realization that Tyler was the other half of her heart, the other part of herself that she had been searching for without knowing it. She had achieved her dream, gained success, but it wasn't until Tyler walked into her life and brought so many emotions alive within her that she had realized what had been missing. How could she go back to life without him?

As they settled along the curb to watch the parade, Tyler leaned down and whispered in her ear.

"You doing okay?"

The fine hairs on the back of her neck tingled as his breath washed across her skin. Emma smiled up at him over her shoulder.

"Yeah, I am, I really am."

His hand squeezed her shoulder, flooding her with warmth and strength. With Tyler beside her, Emma felt capable of taking on the whole world. But what if he left? She tried to shut out the distressing thought, determined to not think about the future. But she couldn't help sending up an urgent plea to the Lord.

Please God, let Tyler stay here in Atlanta. All things are possible with You. I don't believe you put him in my life to yank him back out again. I know it's selfish, but please let him stay.

The parade was longer than Tyler had expected and he found he enjoyed the homemade floats, pulled through the street by four wheel drive pickup trucks or lawn tractors. The Atlanta high school marching band was surprisingly good, and of course there were the veterans and Cub Scouts, both proud in their uniforms. Drill teams on horseback and baton twirlers in their sequin studded leotards went past as firemen threw candy from the back of their truck. Tyler saw how much small town life had to offer, how diverse this community was and yet how connected they were to one another.

Yes, he had seen much bigger parades in the city, but there you didn't hear the firemen saying, "Here Jordan, here's some candy. Bobby, quit hogging it all, let the little ones get some, too." "Hey Ed, Carolynn, great to see you back in town!" "Emma, keep your chin up." The familiar banter went on throughout the parade, townspeople encouraging the little twirlers when they dropped their batons, laughing and joking when the horses in the drill team left a trail of road apples down the middle of the street.

"That's why they put you guys at the end of the parade, eh Steve?" someone in the crowd yelled out to the leader of the drill team and everyone laughed.

Tyler looked down at the dark head in front of him. Emma had laughed and cheered along with the others. He could tell she was trying to enjoy herself, and yet he felt the tension in her whenever anyone squeezed too close, how she pulled away whenever people brushed against them, her eyes looking up frantically until she recognized a face and then relaxed again. He marveled at her bravery, to expose herself to the public after all she had been through in the past week. In the same situation, he wasn't sure he could do the same. He remembered all too well the devastation he had felt after the accident, how he had hidden himself away from the prying eyes of friends, family and strangers. And now here Emma was, scared, true, but willing none the less to face the world. Tyler knew her strength came not from his presence behind her, but from the steel core of faith that she was firmly grounded on.

He looked around him once more, at faces that were quickly growing familiar, and then back down at Emma. How could he leave here, leave her? He had a good job in the city, co-workers waiting for his return, but it held no appeal for him at all. There was absolutely nothing to draw him back to his old life and everything to keep him here in this new life God had opened up for him. Everything except a job. Emma turned suddenly, flashing a smile up at him and instantly worry about the details disappeared. Tyler knew he was staying. He would just have to leave the rest in the good Lord's hands.

* * *

When the parade was finished the crowd dispersed, the majority heading toward the township park where the rest of the day's festivities would be held. Emma found herself carried along on the current of people, Tyler holding firmly to her hand. Once across the street and on the park grounds, the multitude thinned out and Emma was able to catch her breath. She had to admit that the press of people and the sudden feeling of loss of control had momentarily frightened her, but now, with more space around her, she felt the wave of dizzying fear pass.

"So, what now?" Tyler asked.

"Well, the county dignitaries will be doing their speeches pretty soon, then the band will be in the pavilion playing, the VFW is selling hot dogs and pizza over in the community center. There will be a horseshoe tournament and then later the canoe race on the river, then the fireworks. You name it, it's probably going on."

"Emma, I heard there's some lovely craft booths over by the produce market," Carolynn said, stopping by Emma's side. "We're going to walk over and take a quick peek. You want to come?"

Emma slid a sidelong glance at Tyler.

"Not really Mom, but you guys go ahead."

"Are you sure? Will you be okay?"

"Of course I will, I have my bodyguard, remember?" Emma laughed and hooked a thumb toward Tyler. "You go on, we'll catch up with you in a little while."

"Well, if you're sure, honey." Carolynn dropped a quick peck on Emma's cheek. "Be careful."

"Mom, we're in a park full of people. I'll be fine," Emma reassured as her parents moved reluctantly away. "What would you like to do?" She looked up at Tyler. "I've seen all this every year since I was a baby, so you tell me what pricks your interest?"

"How about you, sweetheart." Tyler grinned

down at her and crossed his well muscled arms over his chest. "You definitely prick my interest."

"You've made that abundantly clear, and I'm flattered. But I would think by now you would have realized that I seem to have a penchant for attracting trouble. Maybe we should try to find something else to amuse you for awhile." Emma tried to slow her crazily beating heart. She couldn't seem to control her body's reaction when Tyler looked down at her with those intense green eyes. "You play horseshoes?"

"I highly doubt I would find horseshoes nearly as amusing as I do you. Plus, you are right about that trouble thing and my duty for the day is to keep you out of it. I wouldn't be able to do that if I were busy playing horseshoes." He quirked an eyebrow, curious. "You wouldn't be trying to distract me would you, so that you could slip away and go play detective?"

"Absolutely not!" Emma's words rang with indignation. "I've learned my lesson about that, really I have. I'm leaving the whole situation in Nate's hands. And God's. I realize that I stuck my nose in where it didn't belong, and I could have gotten hurt. I'm not doing that anymore, I promise."

"Good." Tyler dropped an arm around her shoulders and pulled her tightly to his side. "What do you say then that we get something to eat. I'm starved."

The afternoon passed quickly as Emma found herself completely captivated by Tyler's attention. They ate their hot dogs seated across from one another at a picnic table, discussing everything from politics to foreign affairs. Tyler listened to her views with interest.

Emma carefully avoided asking him questions about his past. She didn't want to bring up the subject of his job and risk having to talk about his future plans, him leaving. So she expertly side-stepped personal topics and stuck to safer subjects, like the economy. Tyler was intelligent, rational and so easy to talk to. Emma was amazed as new layers of his personality were revealed. One minute he was boldly flirting with her, enjoying her awkward embarrassment, the next he would be serious, throwing her emotions into disarray.

When the band struck up the music in the pavilion, Tyler took Emma by complete surprise. Grabbing her hands, he flung her away from him, twirling her several times before pulling her back toward himself, moving in perfect time with the music. Emma giggled as he continued to lead her in a series of fancy dance steps.

"Wow, you're quite the dancer." Emma laughed breathlessly as he pulled her once more to his chest.

"Sweetheart, I have moves you can't even imagine." His eyes held a slightly wicked gleam as he once more twirled her under his arm. Emma rolled her eyes dramatically.

"Oh, I think I can imagine alright!"

"Don't bet on it." Tyler became serious as he pulled her back against his chest. He stopped dancing, even though the music continued. He gazed steadily down into Emma's eyes, breathing hard.

Emma could feel the heat emanating from Tyler's body, could feel his heart pounding within his chest where her body rested against his. Her own heart seemed to be beating with the same rapid rhythm. She couldn't pull her eyes away from his, couldn't seem to make herself back away from his solid form.

Tyler's eyes dropped to her lips and Emma knew what was coming, yearned for it. She tipped her chin higher, giving him full access as he slowly lowered his head. Her eyelids drifted closed as he settled his mouth on hers. Bright lights seem to flash behind her closed eyes as Tyler toyed with her lips before applying soft pressure, drawing her closer. Emma was lost in the sensations that washed over her, her mind losing the ability to think of anything else except the pleasure of Tyler's kiss.

A bundle of firecrackers went off behind them. Emma jumped back from Tyler's arms as the air filled with acrid smoke. She covered her still ringing ears.

"Well, that was perfect timing, I must say." Emma smiled up at Tyler as fireworks continued to go off within her stomach.

Tyler laughed and tugged her back into his arms. "Not bad, huh?" His smile was wide as he looked down at her. "Believe me, sweetheart, it's only the beginning."

Besides the fireworks, the annual canoe race on the Thunder Bay river was the most anticipated event of the day. The sun had just begun its slow, westward descent when the canoes lined up across the widest part of the water way, heading downstream toward the dam that funneled the river under County Road 487. The canoes were to pull up on the far shore, across from the park, just before the dam.

Excited townspeople jostled for viewing spots along the banks of the river, ready to cheer on their favorite teams. A loud shout rose from the crowd when the starting pistol sounded and the participants began paddling hard toward the finish line.

The heavy rain that had fallen earlier in the week had swollen the river and it ran fast as the banks narrowed closer to the dam. Emma watched as several canoes jockeyed for position, trying to fight the current and head toward the far shore. The rivals laughed and badgered one another good naturedly, their catcalls carrying across the water.

Two teenagers laughed hysterically as they tried to keep their slender canoe in balance. The girl dropped her paddle and the boy in the back immediately reached into the water at the same time she did. The canoe began to tip precariously. Laughter rang out as the occupants fell into the river. Two heads bobbed up, still laughing.

Momentarily distracted, the pilots of the competing canoe stopped paddling and were immediately swung around by the strong current. Trying to turn toward the far shore, they fought to bring the bow around and gain control. The girl in the water began to swim toward shore as the other canoe swung crazily in the current once more. The pointed metal bow of the canoe hit the girl on the side of the head with a resounding thunk sending her under.

"Brandy!" Emma heard a frantic voice call out as the boy thrashed around in the water, looking for the girl.

"Oh my gosh, it's Kirt!" Emma yelled and grabbed Tyler's arm.

The blond head surfaced farther downstream, the fast current quickly pulling her toward the dam. The girl didn't struggle against the pull, made no move to swim toward shore. As the head disappeared once more beneath the surface, Emma realized the girl was unconscious.

Tyler had the same revelation. In an instant he was out of his tennis shoes and diving into the river. Astounded at his immediate response, Emma watched in terror as Tyler surfaced and began swimming with strong strokes toward the spot where Brandy had disappeared.

The dam formed a narrow artificial waterfall which channeled the water into a sluiceway and under the road. At the bottom of the sluiceway was a large iron grate. If Brandy was unconscious and got sucked into the sluice, the force of the falling water would hold her under, pinned against the grate. Even as strong as Tyler was, Emma couldn't fathom how he would be able to get Brandy out if she fell into the sluice. Emma held folded hands to her lips, praying fervently. She saw Tyler surface and dive again repeatedly, each time coming closer to the dangerous water flowing over the dam.

Firemen and police that had been dispersed throughout the crowd quickly assembled to help in the rescue, several of them lining up along the walkway across the top of the dam. A motor boat was fast approaching from up river and helpless teams in canoes paddled out of the way, the fun of the race now gone.

A sopping Kirt swam to shore. Walking up on the bank, shorts and tank top dripping, he stopped beside Emma. He turned tortured eyes back out on the river, searching for signs of Brandy. Horror stricken, the two of them watched as Tyler fought the current close to the dam. Instinctively Emma reached out a hand and took a tight hold on Kirt's wet arm. She squeezed.

"You'd better start praying hard, Kirt," she said, her voice choked.

"I am Miss Dawson," Kirt replied in a hoarse whisper.

Once more Tyler dove and Emma knew this was his final chance. If he didn't reach Brandy now, the girl would be over the dam and trapped in the sluice and Tyler could very well be sucked under as well, drowned in the thundering water. Every muscle in Emma's body strained toward the river, as if her own strength could bring Tyler back to the surface.

"Please God, please God, please God," Emma whispered repeatedly.

A gasp went up from the crowd as Tyler's head broke the surface of the water. Slowly he began swimming away from the dam, still fighting against the river that wanted to pull him down. Several moments passed before the crowd realized the rescuer swam with only one arm. The other held a limp head above the water. As soon as Tyler reached the shallows, two firemen rushed out to assist him, lifting the unconscious girl and hurriedly splashing up the bank. They laid her on the dry sand as Tyler, breathing hard and dripping, knelt beside them. The three worked in unison to check her vital signs and begin CPR.

The crowd formed a circle, watching in morbid fascination as the men tried to force life back into Brandy's body. Kirt left Emma's side and shouldered his way through the mass of spectators, frantic to reach his girlfriend's side. The wail of an ambulance pierced the gathering dusk, making heads turn.

Emma moved farther away as the ambulance crew hurried down the hill, stretcher in tow. She was overwhelmed by Tyler's heroic action, his willingness to risk his life to save a girl he didn't even know. The truth of what she had just witnessed dealt a hammer blow to Emma's heart. Tyler had his answer now. His ability to react in an emergency was still intact. He would be able to return to the job he loved.

"Excuse me, are you Emma Dawson?" A young woman Emma had never seen before stopped in front of her.

"Yes." Emma turned her attention from the crowd around Tyler to the stranger.

"I was asked to give you this." A white envelope was pressed into her hand and the woman quickly walked up the hill, giving Emma no time to ask questions. Emma's wary eyes followed her. Seeing the woman join a man with a stroller, she relaxed once more.

Curious, she turned the envelope over and opened the flap, pulling out a flowered piece of stationery. Her heart began beating wildly as she read:

Miss Dawson, I need to talk to you right away. I know something that might be useful to you. It's a matter of life and death.

It was signed Doreen Pearson.

Wildly Emma looked around for Tyler. She caught a glimpse of him through the crowd, standing with the ambulance crew that was placing Brandy on a stretcher. A sheriff's deputy was with him. Emma watched Tyler nod, saw him talking earnestly with the officer. She knew there was going to be a lot to sort out about what had taken place. Statements would need to be made.

The ambulance attendants lifted the stretcher and made their way up the hill, Tyler and the other firemen automatically following. Emma looked down once more at the note in her hand, indecision tearing at her. She shouldn't go. It was dangerous. Tyler would kill her. She had promised.

A vision of Doreen's battered face flashed into her mind. A matter of life and death, she said, and Emma could very well believe it. If it was Adam who had put those bruises on his mother's face, she was most definitely in danger. Maybe Doreen wanted to warn her about Adam's next plan. If she could just convince Doreen to go to the police, together the two of them could stop the madness. If it was Adam who was causing it.

Emma looked around one last time. Her parents were in the community center playing pinochle. If she showed them the note, they would insist on calling Nate immediately. Emma knew if she arrived at the Pearson home with a police escort, the woman would clam up tighter than a rusty trap. It was going to take a very delicate touch to get Doreen to come clean about her son.

Mind made up, Emma began winding her way out of the park. She would just dash over there, get whatever information the woman had, and then come back. Tyler would most likely be occupied for awhile yet and now that he was a regular hometown hero, Emma was sure the locals would keep him distracted for some time, wanting to hear all the details of his daring rescue.

Once she talked to Doreen, they would call Nate and this whole thing would be wrapped up, finally. And then Tyler would kill her. She walked quickly across the dam, her eyes falling on the water rushing over the water fall, foaming and churning where it hit the grate at the bottom of the sluice. She shivered uncontrollably at the thought of all that power holding Tyler pinned beneath the water.

Thank you, Lord, that he and Brandy didn't drown down there, she prayed as she hurried over the dam and crossed the road, heading toward the Pearson place.

CHAPTER TWENTY THREE

The sun had nearly set by the time Emma stepped up onto the Pearson's rickety front porch. Surprised by the lateness of the hour, she realized she had to make this quick to get back in time for the fireworks. She gave a hurried knock on the frame of the screen door, shivering as the inner door swung open with an eerie creak.

"I knew you would come," a quiet voice spoke from the darkness, freezing Emma in terror. Too late, she took a step back, retreating from the porch. Her foot had barely made the first step when the screen door flew open and her wrist was captured in a vise-like grip.

"Not so fast, Emma." Mercilessly Adam drug her into the house, surprising Emma with his wiry strength. "The party's just begun, you can't leave yet."

He kicked the front door closed with a foot, brutally pushing Emma up against rough wood. He put a forearm across her throat, pinning her. She tried to kick out at him, but he merely pressed against her harder, leering into her face as he ground his lower body against hers.

"We have some unfinished business to attend to." Adam's foul breath fanned across her cheek, making her want to gag.

"Where's your mother?" Emma managed to ask, her mind still reeling with fear. She had to grasp at something, anything. Adam laughed.

"She's up town, like everyone else, getting ready to watch the fireworks. The whole town is otherwise occupied Emma, even your good friend the deputy. That just leaves me and you. We're gonna have my own brand of fireworks right here."

"Nate will be here any minute. I told him, I told him I was coming here. He knows you've been watching me. He knows you set the fire and destroyed my shop," Emma gasped out, her voice trembling.

"You're a terrible liar. If Nate Sweeney knew it was me, he would have arrested me already. And you didn't tell anybody you were coming here, I watched you. I know all about you Emma, know what a soft heart you have. Ooh, your soft all over huh?" Emma cringed as Adam ran a hand over her body. "But, there will be time enough for that later." Relief washed over her as he removed his hand and reached for something by the door. "I planned for all contingencies, although you are terribly predictable. I really should thank you for making this so easy for me. I almost believe you wanted to be caught."

Emma's relief was short lived as her face was suddenly swathed in scratchy darkness. She began fighting in earnest as the sack was pulled over her head. She kicked out and clawed with her hands as Adam tried to hold her. The scramble sent them both crashing to the floor. In an instant Emma was on her back, Adam straddling her mid section. She went completely still as his hand circled her throat, squeezing, cutting off all oxygen.

"Don't do it Emma," Adam's cruel voice cut through the darkness that had swallowed her. "Don't fight me. I don't want to hurt you, but I will."

Within moments Emma's hands were tied and the burlap sack secured around her neck. Stumbling in the blackness, she was forced out of the house and shoved into the trunk of a car. Oh, God, what had she done?

Tyler. Tyler would find her. He would move heaven and earth to keep her safe. Hope flared to life within her and then quickly died as the car rumbled to life, the exhaust penetrating the cramped trunk. How could Tyler possibly find her? He would have no idea where to look. He had no idea where she had gone, didn't know about Doreen or the note or Adam. The combination of exhaust fumes and claustrophobia made Emma nauseous and her mind swam. Vaguely she recalled Tyler questioning her about Adam. Would he remember the name? *Please Lord*, her fuzzy brain pleaded, *please help him remember, please send Tyler to save me.*

The adrenaline was still pumping fiercely through Tyler's body as he watched the rescue squad crew lift the stretcher bearing a pale and shaken

Brandy into the ambulance. His reaction when he had seen the unconscious girl being pulled down the river had been instinctual. The minute he had recognized the situation, all his training and experience had taken over, as if he hadn't had three months off the job. He felt immense relief, not just because Brandy would live, but because he had the answer to his deepest, darkest question. He would be okay. He would be able to get back in a rescue squad again. The skills that he had worked so hard to master and refine were still there. He was completely healed.

The ambulance doors slammed shut. Kirt watched forlornly as the attendants climbed into the vehicle and drove away, lights flashing.

"She'll be fine." Tyler dropped a comforting hand onto Kirt's bony shoulder.

"She's probably never gonna talk to me again."

"Sure she will. It was an accident, it wasn't your fault. Keep your chin up. Hey, have you seen Emma?" Tyler began scanning the crowd in the park.

"Miss Dawson? Sure, she was down by the river, watching, when you were trying to save Brandy. But I haven't seen her since then, I was too busy watching you." Kirt looked up with hero worship in his eyes.

"Thanks buddy." Tyler gave Kirt's shoulder one last pat then headed down the hill toward the river bank. Dusk was gathering and the crowd was thick, waiting for the fireworks that would be shot off over the water. Though he searched high and low, Tyler didn't see Emma among them.

Tyler racked his brain, finally remembering that Emma's parents were up in the community center playing cards. Sure that's where she would be, he headed up the hill, stopping several times to ask familiar faces if they had seen Emma. Trepidation stole over him as they all shook their head no. He could feel panic gathering as he approached the community center. The card game had long since disbanded, the players distracted by the excitement of a near drowning. He spied Ed and Carolynn standing amid several of their friends. His spirits sank even lower as he realized there was no familiar dark head among them.

"There's the hero!" Ed called out as Tyler approached their group. He held out a hand, grasping Tyler's in a hard shake. "Great job, son."

"It was nothing." Tyler pulled his hand away and looked down at the ground. He scratched the bridge of his nose.

"Nothing?!" one of the locals exclaimed. "We watched the whole thing. You could have been killed in that dam, the girl too. It's a great thing you did, a great thing. It will be the talk of the town, that's for sure." He slapped Tyler's shoulder and the group moved away, leaving him alone with Emma's parents.

"It will be nice for the town to have something else to talk about," Carolynn said emphatically. "Then maybe they'll stop talking about Emma and what's been happening to her. I don't think I could possibly answer another question. I've been sorely tempted to tell people to quit being such busy bodies and mind their own business. Where is Emma, by the way?" She looked expectantly at Tyler.

"Well." He cleared his throat. "Actually, I thought

she would be with you. I lost sight of her, you know, when I dove in the river and I haven't seen her since. I went down there looking for her just now, but didn't see her, so I figured she must be with you."

"You're telling me she's disappeared?" Carolynn's voice rose an octave. "I thought you were supposed to be guarding her!"

"I was, I didn't take my eyes off her all day, until... I reacted automatically, I couldn't just stand there and watch that girl drown!"

"Of course not," Ed reassured. "Carolynn, don't over react. Remember the last time we assumed the worst, she ended up being perfectly safe. Maybe she's in the restroom, or maybe she went home."

"Or maybe she's been kidnapped!" Carolynn was on the verge of hysterics.

"Mrs. Dawson, in order to be kidnapped, Emma would have had to leave the park, she would have had to wander away from the crowd, and why would she do that? She promised me she wouldn't do anything foolish."

"Then why isn't she here? She never would have walked home alone in the dark after what's happened. I'm telling you, something's happened to her. She got lured away, somehow. I know you care deeply for Emma, Tyler, and the one thing you have to know about her is that she all too often thinks with her heart and not with her head."

Tyler shook his own blond head, trying to deny that which was rapidly becoming all too clear.

"She swore to me she was leaving all of this to Sweeney. If she was suspicious of something, she would have gone to him and told him about it."

Carolynn's look held something akin to pity. "I tried to warn you about her stubborn streak. If the opportunity presented itself to her to solve this case, she would totally forget her fear and good sense, and any promises she made to you, and rush right in. She could be the poster child for Murder, She Wrote."

Tyler knew with absolute certainty that Carolynn was right. Just as his instincts had immediately told him that the girl in the river needed help, they were telling him now that Emma was in grave danger. He let out a deep breath.

"Let's go find Sweeney."

Nate was nowhere to be found. The fireworks were about to start and many of the firemen and sheriff's deputies were busy orchestrating the light show and keeping the crowds back a safe distance. The few officers that were patrolling the area had their hands full with people who had had too much to drink and kids with no parental supervision. Their main concern was keeping the people in the park safe and they weren't overly worried about one missing woman.

"She could be anywhere," they were told over and over again. "Maybe she got sick and went home, did you check there? No, well go do that and come back if she's not there."

Frustrated, Tyler finally sent Emma's parents back to her house. He didn't like them going alone, in case someone was lurking there, but he wanted to stay at the park and keep searching. He told them to call the sheriff's office immediately and let them know what was happening. Carolynn rolled her eyes, the Montmorency County police force falling in her estimation with every passing second. As much animosity as he had felt for Nate Sweeney in the past, Tyler had no doubt he would take Emma's disappearance seriously, if they could just get word to him. Sweeney knew the threat was real and would be as concerned for Emma's safety as Tyler was.

After the older couple left the park, Tyler continued trying to turn up clues. He stopped to question complete strangers, describing Emma in detail, asking if they had seen her. Some had, earlier in the day, down by the river, but none remembered seeing her after the rescue. He grew more frantic as each minute ticked off his watch. He had to find Emma, and soon. *Lord, help me!*

"Hey Jesse, this is the guy that saved Brandy." Kirt approached him, dragging his younger friend behind. The two looked at him in astonishment when he grabbed them by the shoulders exclaiming,

"Boys, you are the answer to my prayers!"

Jesse laughed. "You sound like Miz Dawson, she says stuff like that all the time."

"Miss Dawson is exactly who I need to talk to you guys about." Both boys immediately got serious.

"Yeah, what about Miss Dawson?"

"We can't seem to find her anywhere."

"I told you earlier, the last time I saw her was when you were in the river, saving Brandy. What about you, twerp." He looked over at Jesse. "You seen Miss Dawson?" Jesse shook his dark head, anxiety starting to show on his young face.

"Not since last night. Geez Kirt, you don't think it's…"

"Shut up twerp, we promised Miss Dawson we wouldn't say nothin' to nobody."

"But Kirt, she's in danger. She told me so last night. She's not supposed to go anywhere alone cuz someone wants to hurt her, but she didn't think it was, you know."

"Look guys." Tyler tried to smile and relaxed his stance to appear less threatening. "I'll be honest with you. I've, well, I've sort of been in charge of watching Miss Dawson. Not officially, you know, like the police, but as a friend of the family. That's what I was supposed to be doing today, but when you and the girl fell in the river…" He looked pointedly at Kirt. "I jumped in to save Brandy and so wasn't watching Miss Dawson. So, you know, just like you feel like Brandy getting hurt was your fault, I feel like Emma disappearing is my fault."

"So, what can we do to help?" Kirt asked.

"I think you might have some information that could help me find her. The other night, Emma mistakenly let a name slip, someone she had seen watching her, but when I tried to get her to tell me more, she zipped her lip and wouldn't say a word. Told me to forget she ever said anything. What makes me curious is last night, I just happened to overhear a conversation she had with you." The green eyes shifted to Jesse. "She mentioned the same name. I think it's about time someone told me who Adam is."

CHAPTER TWENTY FOUR

After bumping over miles of rough roads, feeling sick and dizzy with exhaust fumes, Emma was thankful when the rumbling car finally came to stop and the engine turned off. She felt the rush of air as the trunk was opened. Adam grabbed her forearm, yanking her roughly upright. She put her tied hands to her swimming head, feeling like she was going to be sick. She forced the feeling down, swaying as she was dragged from the trunk and set on her feet. Twigs snapped underfoot and branches slapped across her bare legs as she was pulled through the darkness, stumbling often in her blindness. Jerking her to a stop, Adam seemed to fumble with something. A door squeaked and once more Emma was pulled forward.

"Sit down," Adam commanded, pushing her hard against rough boards. She sank down onto a cold dirt floor. More rustling until Emma could see dim light through the burlap. Instinctively she pulled away from the hands at her neck, until she realized Adam was untying the rope that kept her in darkness. He pulled the sack over her head.

A flashlight sat on a crude wooden box in the corner, illuminating the small shack and reflecting the glittering wickedness in Adam's eyes. He squatted down in front of her, an ugly smile twisting his mouth.

"Go ahead and scream, if you want to. No one will hear you. There's nobody around for miles and miles."

Emma's eyes darted around the cramped confines as her mind scrambled to think clearly.

"He's got this little hideout, out by Lake 15. He thinks he's really something having a hideout," Jesse's voice echoed from the past. That must be where they were.

"We can't be that far from town, we didn't drive for that long," Emma said bravely.

"Far enough. No one knows about this place, so even if there are people out looking for you, they won't find you. I have plenty of time to do what I want." He ran a finger down her cheek, chuckling when she tried to turn her face away from him.

"You're so uptight, so holier than thou. I bet you've never had anyone give it to you real good."

"Adam, the Bible says…"

"Shut up!" he growled. Grabbing her once more by the throat, he leaned close, seeming to gain courage from the fear Emma couldn't hide. "Your preaching won't do any good with me, so don't waste your breath." He gave a final squeeze to her abused throat before shoving away from her and rising to his feet. He went to the door and peered out at the night.

"It's true though, you know, what the Bible says," Emma stated in a quiet voice.

"I thought I told you to shut up." Satisfied that they were still alone, Adam came back and hunkered down in front of her again. "Actually, I do want you to talk. I want you to tell me how it felt, Miss High-and-mighty, to see your perfect little world crumpled up like so much garbage. What exactly went through your mind each time I took another precious piece of your fairy tale life? How did you like it, going from having everything to having nothing? Maybe it finally got your fancy panties in a knot, huh?"

Pity for this lost soul replaced Emma's fear, and the deep hatred she had felt for him just this morning evaporated. This was who she had wanted dead? This poor shell of a boy?

"Is that what you've felt like, since your father left? Like your life went from everything to nothing?"

"This isn't about me!" Adam's eyes were cold and Emma knew she had hit close to the mark. "It's about you, Miss Goody-goody. You with Kirt and Jesse following you around like pathetic, love sick puppies."

"They're nice boys."

"Nice." His face twisted in a sneer and he reached a hand to touch her. "We both know I'm not nice, don't we?"

Emma tried to ignore the revulsion that washed over her at Adam's touch.

"You know Adam, you think you've taken things from me, but the Bible says the things of this world will pass away. It's what we have in heaven that really matters. Even though you burned down my garage, even though you destroyed my shop, even if," she stumbled on the words but forced herself to continue. "Even if you rape me, and kill me, it doesn't matter. This life is just a pit stop on the way to where I'm going."

A rumbling like thunder rolled across the sky and shook the rickety shanty. Emma and Adam both looked around in surprise as the ground seemed to shake again and then again. It took several moments for Emma to recognize the booming sound. The fireworks. If they could hear them this clearly, they couldn't be that far from town.

"I know you feel your father abandoned you, Adam. But you have a Heavenly Father who says He will never leave you nor forsake you. You feel alone and unloved, but Jesus loves you, loves you so much that He died for your every sin. Even this, right now, can be forgiven. Maybe you think you've gone too far this time, like you can't turn back, but that isn't true. You can still stop this. If you repent and ask to be forgiven, God will do it, for Jesus' sake.

"It's like, if the police do come." Oh Nate, please come, Emma sent up the silent plea. "If the police come and you get arrested and go to court, you'll have a lawyer to plead your case. Jesus is like our lawyer. He pleads our case in the court of heaven. Whatever we've done wrong, no matter how awful, He stands before God and says 'My blood has paid the price for this crime' and God proclaims us innocent."

Adam said nothing. He sat down cross-legged on the dirt. Resting his chin in the palm of his hand, he continued to stare at her, thinking. Emma took heart and continued.

"You can do that right now, Adam, and God will forgive you of this sin. More than that, He'll renew your heart and life and mind. He'll take away all this pain and hatred that you feel."

Adam's eyes narrowed as he thought.

"If your God is so great, why hasn't He saved you from me?" he asked.

"He will, He will." Emma leaned her head back against the rough boards and closed her eyes. "Even if I die, yet will I live."

"So, this Adam, do you think he would hurt Emma?" Tyler asked Kirt and Jesse, after they had explained about the outcast boy and how he had been seen watching Emma. Kirt shrugged.

"He's strange, and he can be mean, but I don't know if he would actually hurt somebody," Kirt said.

"I think he would," Jesse stated his opinion. "I don't like him, he gives me the creeps, and I think he gave Miz Dawson the creeps, too. Even though she's nice and tried to pretend it didn't bother her, I could tell he was givin' her the willies. There's somethin' about him that just isn't right. I could see him leavin' those dead flowers and settin' fire to her garage. He's one of them people who just seems completely empty inside."

"If he did take Emma, where do you think he

would go?" Tyler asked.

"Him and his mom live on Airport Road, just over there." Kirt pointed through the darkness, across the river.

"Let's go then." Tyler started walking but both boys held back. He turned and looked at them. "I'm going to need your help. The cops are all busy and they aren't too worried about Emma being gone. They've got other concerns right now. All you've got to do is show me the way, okay, and we'll trust the Lord for the rest."

Kirt and Jesse looked at each other. Kirt straightened taller and Jesse followed his friend's example.

"Okay, we'll show you where he lives. I hope my mom doesn't find out about this or I'm in big trouble," Kirt said, leading the way through the park and across the dark road.

It took only minutes for the three to reach the run down house. No light showed in the windows, no sign that anyone was about.

"Do you think he's in there?" Jesse whispered to Tyler as the three stood at the edge of the yard, hidden in the shadow of the trees.

"I don't know, Jesse. You boys wait here while I go around and see if I can hear anything or look in the windows."

The boys did as they were told, watching as Tyler bent over at the waist and stealthily made his way across the yard. It didn't take long for him to make the short trip around the house. He came back shaking his head.

"I didn't see or hear anything. I'm going to go up

and try the door, but I don't think anyone's in there."

Tyler made his way quietly to the rickety porch. He climbed over the creaky steps and stopped at the front door. Gently he opened the screen, grimacing at the squeak that seemed amplified in the quiet night. The front door wasn't latched and swung inward with a slight push from Tyler's fingertips. He stuck his head into the room, listening.

Knowing with a sinking heart that the house was empty, he entered, wondering if he could get arrested for trespassing. He wasn't a policeman and had no right to be going into someone's home. But Tyler cared about none of the legalities, his only concern was finding Emma.

Running his hand over the wall, Tyler felt a light switch and clicked it on. The shabby room was illuminated in dim yellow light. Quickly his eyes scanned the walls, the furniture, the floor. A flash of color in the drab room caught his eye. Squatting down he reached out to pick it up; red and blue hair ribbons still tied in a bow. Emma had been here, she had obviously struggled with someone, enough to loosen the ribbons from her hair. In a blur of motion, Tyler stood, flipped off the lights and left the house, jumping the short distance off the porch and jogging to where the boys still stood.

"She was here." He held the ribbons out to show the boys. "But the house is empty now. Where could he have taken her?"

"I think I know." Jesse looked up, his eyes alight with hope and excitement. "He's got a hideout. Remember Kirt, I told you and Miz Dawson about it last week. Remember, you were mad cuz I hadn't told you about it before."

"Where, Jesse, where is the hideout?" Tyler leaned down and looked closely into the boy's face, urgency galloping like a race horse through him.

"Out at Lake 15. I can show you."

The three began jogging in the direction of Emma's house. Tyler sent Kirt inside to tell Emma's parents to inform Nate of their suspicions. Not bothering to go inside himself, Tyler jumped into his truck as Jesse climbed in the passenger side. With a squeal of tires, Tyler did a U turn in the middle of the street and shot out of town, praying they would get to Emma before Adam did her any more harm.

At the entrance to the campground, Tyler slowed. He turned off the truck's headlights as he turned in and crept all too slowly up the sandy lane, only the orange glow of the parking lights guiding him.

"You better stop here," Jesse said. "The campground's just through there. He could see us coming, or hear the truck."

Tyler pulled over to the side of the road and cut the engine. The two sat in silence for a moment.

"Okay, Jesse, where exactly is this hideout?"

"It's up on the ridge." Jesse pointed. "But we have to go into the campground part first. I don't think I could find it from here, not in the dark."

They opened their doors and climbed out.

"Don't slam your door," Tyler reminded.

"I won't," Jesse whispered back.

Like thieves in the night, the two crept down the dusty road, the pale moonlight guiding the way.

Tyler kicked a pebble and cringed as it bounced along in front of them, sounding like gunshot in the silence. A concrete post marked the entrance to the campground, a wooden sign announcing that it was closed. Tyler and Jesse stopped, peering through the darkness all around.

"I don't see a car." Tyler's shoulders slumped in disappointment. What if this was a wild goose chase?

"There's lots of two tracks and logging roads and ATV trails all over the woods, he wouldn't have to park down here," Jesse reassured. "Yeah, I'm pretty sure there's a trail up there toward the top of the ridge, it comes out farther down the road, closer to your place. He could have gone that way and parked his car up at the top, figuring it wouldn't be seen."

"Okay, let's go find out if he's up there. Think you can do it?" Tyler looked at the young boy's face, wan in the darkness. Jesse bravely squared his shoulders.

"Yeah, for Miz Dawson, I can do it. For her, I'd do just about anything."

Tyler gave him an encouraging pat on the back to start him forward. He agreed completely. He would do anything to get Emma back in his arms again, safe and sound.

The sound of exploding fireworks made them both jump, stopping to look heavenward. The distant rumbling came again and again. Tyler smiled. Perfect timing. Nothing like a drum roll to go along with Hollywood heroics.

* * *

"Enough small talk, it's time." Adam lifted himself from the dirt and moved to the small wooden box in the corner. He took out a tattered blanket, shaking it out and laying it on the hard ground. He shot Emma a wicked grin. "Don't want you getting all dirty, you know."

"Adam you don't have to do this."

Pain shot through her as he grabbed her arms and hauled her to her feet. Nails dug into the tender flesh of her upper arms as he leered into her face.

"I know you're probably saving yourself for marriage, but don't worry. There's not going to be any marriage, so why not enjoy yourself a little before you meet your Maker, huh?"

"Why, Adam, why do you hate me so much? What have I ever done to you?" Hot tears burned her eyes as Emma fought to keep them hidden, not wanting to show any weakness and give him more pleasure.

"You've never done anything to me," Adam admitted, his voice low. "You've never given me the time of day. Why would you? You with your perfect house and your perfect shop and your perfect friends and your perfect deputy. That's what I can't figure out." A puzzled expression crossed his face. "Where does the guy with the scar fit into your perfect picture? I didn't think you would dirty your lily white hands with someone so disfigured."

"Tyler's not disfigured. He's handsome and smart and good and kind. You've got it all wrong, Adam. I'm not perfect and I'm not looking for perfection in my life."

"Then why would you never look at me?" Adam shook her. "Why would you cross to the other side of the street if you saw me coming? Why didn't you ever ask me to pick blueberries for you." Hurt and resentment built with every word until in a final burst of anger, Adam kicked her legs out from under her. Emma went down hard, falling on her back onto the blanket. Adam was immediately on top of her, straddling her hips.

"I know I'm not good enough. I wasn't good enough for my father to stay. My mom told me enough times how bad I was. Now I'm going to prove it, to you and the rest of the world. Everything that's ever been said about me, everything you've ever thought about me, you were right."

He reached to begin unzipping his jeans.

"I'm sorry Adam, I hope you can forgive me."

Emma's words stilled his hands.

"What did you say?"

"I said I was sorry. You're right, I have thought bad things about you, and your family. I've passed judgement, instead of reaching out to you and your mom in Christian love. What you said is true, in a lot of ways. My life has been completely different from yours and I can see where you would think I'm a snob. I've probably given that impression to a lot of people. I hope you can forgive me."

"You're just saying that, trying to sweet talk me out of what I'm going to do. It won't work." Adam went back to working his zipper.

Laying there on the hard ground, Emma's sense

of helplessness began to evaporate. She had done the best she could, said all she could say, now she was no longer content to lay here and allow Adam to ruin her. Maybe she couldn't stop it, but she would die fighting.

"Okay Adam, if you're determined to do this awful thing, then I hope you won't mind if I do this." The rumbling of a firework rolled away. Emma took a deep breath, opened her mouth and screamed as loud as her voice box would allow. The piercing shriek seemed to bounce off the flimsy walls of the shack and echo into the night beyond.

"Shut up!" Adam fell forward, covering her mouth with his dirty hand. "I told you screaming wouldn't do you any good!"

Emma's tied hands were trapped between their bodies, but she used all her strength to buck and roll sideways, trying to unseat Adam from atop her. His hand slipped as he fought to keep her still. She took a quick breath and let out another scream, which he cut off quickly. One hand over her mouth, the other found her throat, his strong fingers squeezing.

"Stop fighting Emma, stop it!"

CHAPTER TWENTY FIVE

Tyler and Jesse made their slow way up the ridge. The canopy of trees blocked out the moonlight and the two had to pick their way carefully. Every snapping twig, every dislodged rock that rolled down the hill had them both ducking for cover. The report of an exploded firework had just faded away in the distance when a woman's scream rent the night. Tyler's heart leapt to his throat as blood hammered through his veins. No longer caring about noise, he ran the last steps up the ridge. Another cry pierced the darkness, cut off suddenly. Frantic, Tyler looked left and right, searching the woods. His eyes, adjusted now to the darkness, caught the small glow of light coming from between warped boards. Adrenaline pumping, he lunged toward the shanty, bursting through the flimsy door.

In a blur of rage his brain registered Emma lying on the ground, the boy on top of her, hands at her throat. Reflex drove him forward, knocking Adam to the side. In an instant Tyler had his own hands around the young man's throat. Terrified dark eyes looked up at him.

"Tyler, no, no, you'll kill him. Tyler don't, please, he's just a kid!" Emma's frantic voice cut through the heavy fog of anger, bringing Tyler to his senses.

Breathing heavily, he loosened his hold on Adam's throat.

"They're here! The cops are here!" Jesse stuck his head in the shack, eyes going wide at the sight inside. "I'll show them up."

"Are you okay." Tyler swung his gaze to Emma, who scooted quickly away from him. "Did he hurt you?"

Her hands automatically went to her bruised neck, but she shook her head.

"No, no he really didn't."

Footsteps pounded up the hill, branches snapping with loud cracks as Jesse led the police to the rickety deer blind. Nate's head was the first to peer through the door.

"Oh, Nate!" Tyler watched in agony as Emma jumped from the ground and threw herself at the deputy. Nate's arms closed around her in a quick hug, then held her away as glittering, blue eyes raked her up and down.

"You okay, Emmy?"

"Yeah, I'm okay." She nodded. "Untie me, please?"

She backed a step away, holding out her tied hands. Nate quickly untied the knot and unwound the rope. When the binding hand fallen away, he assessed the situation inside the shanty, his eyes falling on Tyler who still had Adam pinned.

"Thanks, McGillis. I think you can let him go now. Don't think he'll be hurting anybody any more." Nate entered the cramped confines as Emma slipped around him and out the door. Tyler stood, leaving Adam Pearson to the mercy of the law.

A handcuffed Adam was led down the hill, flanked by two officers. He was put into the back of a patrol car, the slamming door seeming to magnify the simple truth that the danger was now over. Tyler stood with Nate and Emma, feeling tired and defeated. His mind replayed the vision of Emma throwing herself at Nate when he arrived.

"Can you let Emma's parents know that she's with me?" Two pairs of surprised eyes turned to him.

"She'll need to come in and make a statement," Nate informed.

"I know. I'll bring her to the station in just a little while."

"Emma's been through enough for one night, don't you think?" Nate protested. Emma laid a gentle hand on his arm. Tyler's eyes narrowed at the gesture.

"It's okay, Nate. I know I'm safe with Tyler and, and," she hesitated, "we have some things to discuss."

Without another word, Tyler turned and walked to his truck, Emma following. When they were seated in the cab, a sad sigh escaped him and he made no move to turn the key in the ignition. He glanced over at Emma. Her hair was a mess, her braid half undone and wild strands rioted all around her head. Dirt smudged her clothes and face, and yet he thought she was the most beautiful thing on earth. Tyler wanted to wrap her in his arms, to feel her warmth seep deep into his bones, to feel her heart beating next to his and know she was alive. He didn't reach for her. Instead, he looked back out the windshield and started the truck, feeling as if his scars had opened up once more and left him bleeding.

The trembling began, deep in the pit of Emma's stomach and flowed up from her deepest core to run down her limbs. In the silence of the pickup she tried to contain it, but her body continued to shake and her teeth began to chatter. She thought she was going to be sick.

Tyler was angry with her. She could feel the hostility radiating across the truck seat and striking her hard in the heart. Emma knew he had every right to be mad, disappointed. She had acted like a fool after she had promised she wouldn't do anything stupid. Could she really expect him to understand and forgive her?

"You sure you're okay?" Tyler slid a glance across the cab.

"Yes," Emma managed to say between chattering teeth.

"We're almost at the cabin, we'll be there in a minute."

Emma could only nod, waiting, wondering what would happen once they were alone and he confronted her with her own stupidity. Tremors continued to wash over her, making her body spasm continually, no matter how hard she tried to stop it. She was safe now. Then why couldn't she stop shaking? And why did she feel like her life was coming to an end, instead of having a new beginning?

Weeds slapped against the sides of the truck as Tyler pulled into the cabin's driveway. He cut the ignition and sat there in silence. Emma clutched her hands together, trying to curtail their trembling.

"Do you need to go to the hospital?" Tyler's rough voice sliced through the silence that had fallen thick and heavy between them. "Do you need a doctor or anything? I mean, did he, you know..." he let the sentence trail off.

Emma shook her head sadly. "No, no, he didn't. He was going to, before you came."

"Blast it, Emma!" Tyler's hand came down hard, hitting the steering wheel and making Emma jump in her seat. "Why did you do it? You promised me! Promised me! Does that mean nothing to you? Why didn't you tell me about Adam? Or Nate? You could have been...oh forget it!" Reaching for the door handle, Tyler pushed so hard the door swung wide, then ricocheted back toward him. He stuck his foot out, stopping the door as he slid from the truck and stomped toward the cabin.

Several seconds ticked off the clock before Emma opened her door and climbed down from the seat. Full of remorse, she walked toward the cabin on still unsteady legs. When she entered, Tyler stood in the living room, hands on hips, staring into the cold fireplace.

"I'm sorry, Tyler." He didn't turn around. "I

thought it was Doreen, Adam's mom, asking me to come see her. I never thought it was Adam, laying a trap. Honestly I didn't. But." She squared her shoulders and admitted the truth. "I knew it was wrong. I knew you would be angry, but I did it anyway. Please, please forgive me?"

Tyler still held his stiff back to her.

"You told me you didn't love Nate Sweeney."

"What?" Confusion rattled over her. What did Nate have to do with this? "I don't. He's a friend, a good friend. That's all."

"You ran to him though, tonight, when he got there." Tyler turned and all his pain was shining in his eyes. The hurt was so sharp that Emma wanted to turn away from it, but could not. She took a step toward him but he held up a hand, as if to keep her at bay.

"All I could think of was getting to you, finding you. It tore me up inside when I didn't know where you were. Then when I found these." He reached a hand into his front jeans pocket and held out her hair ribbons. His fist closed around the silky material. "You'll never know what went through my mind, how scared I was at the thought of losing you. If he would have, if that kid would have, well." Unable to go on, Tyler just shook his head. "I don't know what I would have done. And then, I get to you and what do you do, run to Nate!"

"Tyler, no," Emma pressed a shaking hand to her lips. "I'm sorry, it's not what it looked like. You were a little occupied, you know, and well, I knew you would be angry with me. My running to Nate, it's not what you think, honestly. I was just so happy to see you both, to be safe, and I wanted out of that shack. I knew you would find me. In my heart I knew God would lead you to me. But I was afraid of what would happen because I knew I had broken your trust. Please forgive me Tyler, please." Her tears were flowing freely now as she closed the small space between them.

"I love you. I've tried not to. I've told myself over and over that you're leaving, and loving you can only bring more pain. But it's the truth. I don't deserve your forgiveness, but I'm asking for it just the same. Please Tyler, believe me, I don't love Nate, I love you."

A large hand came up, a finger tenderly tracing the bruises that circled her throat.

"He hurt you, I wanted to kill him for that."

"No." Emma shook her head and looked up at him. "I hurt myself, really. And I hurt you, I know that. You warned me that my stubbornness would get me in trouble, but I didn't listen. I can't blame you, if you've changed your mind about me. It's probably better that way, really, since you aren't staying." The tears began again.

"Shhhh." Emma found herself caught up in Tyler's strong arms, drawn hard against his chest. "Who said I wasn't staying?"

She felt his lips against her hair, felt his hands drifting over her as if reassuring himself that nothing was broken. Her heart seemed to dangle from a delicate thread as his words sunk in.

"You saved Brandy. You have your answer now. You can go back to your job without fear."

"Yeah, I suppose I could. But since meeting you, the city doesn't seem to hold much charm for me anymore. I really like it here a lot more." He gave he a squeeze for emphasis.

"Could you stay? Would you?" She leaned back in his arms, looking up into his chiseled face, loving the way his eyes searched hers, loving even the scar that ran its way down his cheek. She couldn't keep her hand from straying there, running her fingers over the ridge of pink skin. Tyler leaned into her touch.

"Could and would." He leaned his forehead against hers. "If it's God's will, there will be a way."

"But what about, I mean, can you forgive me then." Emma held her breath, waiting for his answer.

"Yes, sweetheart, I forgive you. But from now on, can we agree, no more making promises we can't keep."

"Okay," the word was carried on a gentle breath as Tyler's lips descended over hers. Emma felt herself lifted, flying on the clouds as she was carried along on the high tide of love. She thought she heard angels singing "hosanna's" as Tyler drew her closer to himself.

Tyler lifted his head to look down at her then cleared his throat and purposely set her away from himself.

"Well, now that we have that settled, I have to get you in to the police station so you can make your statement and we can put this whole mess behind us."

"Okay," Emma smiled. "And Tyler, I do love you. That's a promise."

"I love you too, Emma." Tyler drew her into his arms once more and nuzzled her ear. "That's a promise I intend to keep forever."

Emma was going stir crazy. For days she hadn't been allowed to go anywhere except the police station and the doctor's office. Her mother hovered around, mercilessly forcing her to drink hot tea with honey and lemon to soothe her throat. Many of the locals stopped to visit, reassuring themselves that Emma was fine.

Emma was amazed and grateful for the love and support that, for so many years, she had taken for granted. An army of people had volunteered to clean up the mess from her burned garage and pledged to help her rebuild. Her heart overflowed with love for all these dear people.

"Emma, you aren't going to believe this!" Tyler burst through the front door, skidding to a halt in front of the sofa. Emma giggled and looked up at him. "Is God the coolest, or what?"

"Oh, He's definitely the coolest." She smiled. "After all, He brought me you."

"Well, yeah, that was pretty cool." He grinned and pulled her to her feet. "But this is almost as good. I might have a job!"

"Oh, Tyler, really?"

"Yep. Seems I made a mighty fine impression on some powerful people when I pulled Brandy from the river." He wiggled his eyebrows up and down as he looked at her, causing Emma to giggle again. "There could be a position opening up with the tri-county

EMT service. It's very, very possible that I'll get it!"

Emma threw her arms around his neck, catching Tyler's excitement.

"That's wonderful! You're right, God is pretty amazing! Now you'll have to stay."

"Sweetheart, wild horses couldn't drag me away." He started to laugh.

"What's so funny."

"It just occurred to me, I came up here to get away, thought maybe I'd do a little fishing, and I got caught."

"You sure did. And you're definitely a keeper." Emma's giggle was caught in her throat as Tyler's lips captured hers in a long, deep kiss.

"I think I like getting caught," he whispered as he raised his head.

"That's good, cuz I like catching you. None of that catch and release stuff for me though, no sir. Now that my hook's in you, your stuck with me."

"I think I can handle that." Tyler dropped a quick kiss on her nose. "Now, how about we celebrate by going out to lunch?"

"I'd love it! I haven't been allowed out of the house in forever."

"Great, let's go."

Tyler waited by the door as Emma slipped into her white tennis shoes. He held her hand as they left the porch. When Emma turned toward his truck, he tugged her along the sidewalk instead.

"We're not driving?" she asked

"Nuh-uh," he shook his head. "I feel like walking."

Emma fell into step beside him but when they

came to the corner, she balked as Tyler turned toward the Spot of Tea.

"Where are we going?"

"It's a surprise." Tyler looked down at her and Emma's heart did a triple flip at the love that flowed from his eyes.

"Tyler, I don't want to go this way. There's nothing down there, no other places to eat. I'm not ready yet to…" Emma looked away from him as her imagination conjured up the destruction that had been left inside her shop. She wasn't ready yet to face her once successful business.

"It's okay Em, trust me. Come on."

He gave her no choice but to follow as he held tightly to her hand and crossed the street. Emma's heart beat heavier with each step that took them closer to the Spot of Tea.

"Close your eyes," he commanded, as they stopped in front of the plate glass door.

"Tyler, I don't want to do this. This isn't funny."

"Please, Em." He framed her face with his large hands, his thumbs stroking her cheeks. "Don't be stubborn. For once, trust someone else for a change."

His eyes locked on hers, silently pleading. He was right, she had to learn to trust him more and fight him less. With a resigned sigh, she closed her eyes.

"Okay, they're closed. Are you happy now?"

"Happier than you'll ever know, sweetheart." Tyler once more took her hand and led her inside the shop. She felt as he moved around behind her and put both hands over her eyes. "Ready?" Emma wasn't but didn't say so.

"Ta da!" Tyler dropped his hands.

"Surprise!" Emma's eyes flew open as a multitude of voices yelled out.

There stood her parents, the Delands and Rhonda, Nate Sweeney and Lydia Ebersol, even Kirt and Jesse. Emma's eyes swept around the shop in disbelief. Everything was in place. The tables and chairs were set in front of the windows, covered with spotless, starched linens. Delicate vases holding miniature roses were centered on each table. The glass fronted case was stocked with baked goods.

"What do you think?" Tyler asked as he stood behind her, hands on her shoulders.

"I can't believe it." Emma could feel the tears gather as her throat burned. "How, who?" The gathered crowd laughed.

"Everyone did it, for you. They all pitched in."

Through a haze of tears, Emma saw her mother step forward, felt the familiar arms surround her.

"You know what they say, you can't keep a good man down. A good woman, either. Although Lord knows we tried for the last few days!" Carolynn laughed and kissed Emma's cheek. "You never have made it easy on a person. I hope Tyler knows what he's getting himself in to."

Emma sniffed as her mother moved back and Tyler wrapped his strong arms around her from behind.

"Don't worry, Mrs. Dawson. My eyes are wide open. I believe God will make me equal to the challenge." Emma felt his chuckle seep from her back and settle straight in her heart.

"I'm not that bad, am I?" she protested light-heartedly.

"Actually, yes, I think you are." Tyler turned her, laughing. Emma's face took on an exaggerated pout. "Stubborn as a mule, but we've got a lifetime to work on that. I think I'm going to love every minute of it. And I plan to keep you so busy you'll never have time to play detective ever again."

Catcalls and whistles went up from the assembled crowd as Tyler pulled her into his arms and kissed her full on the mouth.

"I promise, I'll change," Emma said when her lips were free.

"Remember, we agreed, no more promises you can't keep." He gave her a broad grin and a wink. "Besides, life would be awfully boring if you started actually doing what I asked of you. And now that I'm a full-blown hero, I've got my own damsel in distress that I can rescue any time I want."

"So, that's what you think, huh?" Emma stood with hands on hips. "I have to wonder, when all is said and done and we look back on this whole thing, just who saved who?" Her chin went up in its familiar stubborn tilt. Tyler laughed and dropped an arm around her shoulder, turning her back once more to view her restored shop.

"No doubt about it sweetheart, you saved me. And praise God, Jesus saved us all. Now come on, lets go thank everyone for their hard work, and don't go getting riled that they didn't let you in on it."

"I'm not riled, Tyler. I'm thankful. More thankful than you'll ever know. God's given us both second chances. I told you He would use the bad for good, somehow, and He did. I might fail, you might fail, but one thing we can hold fast to, God's promises never fail. He keeps His promises."

Emma moved farther into the room, greeting each person, gratefully accepting their hugs and encouragement. Awestruck she went into the kitchen, opening cupboards to reveal shelves of antique china. Everything sparkled with the cleanliness of a new start, a fresh beginning. She couldn't hold back the tears as she realized fully the sacrifice the people around her had made. Across the room her tearful gaze met Tyler's and he gave her a smile brimming with love.

Thank you Lord, Emma prayed. *I'll do my best to love Tyler as You would have me love him. I know I'll make mistakes, but I'll do the best I can. With You, I know that's a promise I'll be able to keep.*

THE END

Coming soon, PENNY FROM HEAVEN, book 2 in the Northwoods Adventures Series.

Wildlife biologist Pennelope Scott hopes her transfer to Atlanta will mean a new start to her life, but those hopes are quickly dashed when she clashes with newly promoted Sergeant Nate Sweeney upon arrival in town. Nate is intrigued by the beautiful Penny, but her hatred and mistrust of men is quickly evident. What has caused the wariness that Nate sees in Penny's eyes?

Penny is determined to avoid Nate at all cost, but in a town as small as Atlanta, that proves more difficult with each passing day. When Penny stumbles upon a ring of poachers preying on Atlanta's prized elk herd, she knows she should confide in Nate, but the deep-seated pain from her past prohibits her from trusting the handsome officer of the law.

Will Nate be able to scale the wall that Penny has built around her heart? And will Penny be able to save the elk herd or will she fall victim to the poachers before she can confess her growing feelings for Nate? Find out in PENNY FROM HEAVEN, the second book in the Northwoods Adventures Series.

Printed in the United States
28151LVS00001B/88-222